TREASURES OF GRACE
Great Fast

Linking the Readings

Archdeacon Banoub Abdou

Foreword by His Eminence Metropolitan Youssef

Translated by St. Mary & St. Demiana Convent

Treasures of Grace—Great Fast—Linking the Readings
Compendium by Archdeacon Banoub Abdou
Translated by the St. Mary and St. Demiana Convent

Designed by the St. Mary and St. Demiana Convent.

Published by:
The Parthenos Press
101 S Vista Dr, Sandia, TX 78383
stmabbeypress.com

CONTENTS

Foreword by His Eminence Metropolitan Youssef 8

Ninevites' Fast
- Monday 12
- Tuesday 17
- Wednesday 21
- Feast 25

Leave-Taking
- Saturday 29
- Sunday 32

Chart Ninevites' and Leave-Taking days 36

First Week
- Monday 37
- Tuesday 42
- Wednesday 46
- Thursday 50
- Friday 54
- Saturday 58
- Sunday 61

Chart Week #1 Preparing for the Struggle 65

Second Week
- Monday 67
- Tuesday 72
- Wednesday 76
- Thursday 81
- Friday 86
- Saturday 91
- Sunday 94

Chart Week #2 Nature of the Struggle 99

Third Week
- Monday 101
- Tuesday 106

Wednesday 110
Thursday 115
Friday 119
Saturday 125
Sunday 128
Chart Week #3 Purity of the Struggle 132

Fourth Week
Monday 133
Tuesday 137
Wednesday 142
Thursday 147
Friday 152
Saturday 157
Sunday 160
Chart Week #4 Credo of the Struggle 164

Fifth Week
Monday 166
Tuesday 171
Wednesday 176
Thursday 182
Friday 187
Saturday 193
Sunday 197
Chart Week #5 Goal of the Struggle 201

Sixth Week
Monday 203
Tuesday 207
Wednesday 212
Thursday 217
Friday 222
Saturday 234
Sunday 237
Chart Week #6 Anointing of the Struggle 242

Seventh Week
- Monday 243
- Tuesday 248
- Wednesday 253
- Thursday 258
- Friday 262
- Saturday 268
- Sunday 273

Chart Week #7 Victory of the Struggle 275

Appendix 1: Quick Reference Guide 277

Foreword

Annually, there are five *Katameros* books in the Coptic Orthodox Church. *Katameros* (καθ' ἡμέραν) is a Greek word found 45 times in the Holy Bible that means "from day to day" or "daily." Thus, *Katameros* refers to the allotted liturgical readings according to each day. Each book serves a specific season: The Great Fast, Holy Week, Holy Fifty-Days, Annual days, and Annual Sundays. The church was very purposeful in her choice for each day's readings. In his work, published in 1958, Archdeacon Banoub Abdou (1900–1967) attempted to shed light on this wisdom.

The readings for each liturgical day begin with the chanting of the Gospel on the previous evening during the Evening Raising of Incense (that is, Vespers). Each Gospel reading is always accompanied, or rather preceded, by the chanting of the psalm (usually only one verse or a couple of verses). The next morning, another Psalm–Gospel pairing is chanted during the Matins Raising of Incense. Before this Psalm–Gospel set, a unique feature for the Great Fast is the reading of the prophecies. Later, during the catechesis (the Liturgy of the Word), a passage from the Pauline Epistles (the 14 epistles written by Saint Paul) is followed by the Catholic Epistle (a select passage taken from James–Jude), which is then followed by a passage from the Book of Acts. The Acts is followed by the Synaxarium, the chronicles of the saints (not addressed here). A third Psalm–Gospel set concludes the catechetical readings. Another unique feature on the Sundays of the Great Fast is the "Sunday Evening Raising of Incense," where another Psalm–Gospel set is chanted.

In his compendium, Archdeacon Banoub Abdou begins each day "Linking the Readings" where he gives an overall summary linking all the day's readings, highlighting the connecting themes between the prophecies, Gospels, and the epistles. Next, he goes deeper to focus on each in more detail. He first treats the prophecies (during the Ninevites' Fast and Feast, each day only one prophecy is read from the book of Jonah). Next, he addresses the Gospels; the psalm usually expands upon the accompanying Gospel. He groups and treats all the Psalm–Gospel sets before finally turning to the Epistle readings, which is a slight variation from the order followed during the Divine Liturgy. The Archdeacon then includes a sermon on each of the Gospel readings. This volume, published specifically to help the reader link the readings, a cliff-notes version of sorts, does not include these sermons; separate volumes in this series are under publication that include these sermons.

The *Katameros* for the Great Fast incorporates (and begins with) the readings for Jonah's Fast, or rather the Fast of the Ninevites. One might ask what this fast has to do with the Great Fast, but first let us address the idea of fasting and why the Great Fast is so significant. When God created Adam and Eve in the Garden of Eden, they (and their descendants) lived as strict vegans and so they each lived hundreds of years. After the flood, when *new* items were introduced into the human diet, the lifespan began to decrease, and the human nature changed from gardener to hunter. In fasting, we are seeking to return to not only the diet, but also the obedient life Adam lived in the Garden of Eden. In fasting, we are exerting self-discipline by saying "No" to ourselves. We are depriving ourselves of something we want, remembering the times we took or did something we should not; we are making up for our sins. This is what the Ninevites did, they repented from their sins by abstaining from all food (not just eating strict vegan food), and in three days God relented and did not destroy their city (Jonah 3).

The church always arranges for this three day fast to begin two weeks before the Great Fast, as a prelude, because, as the Lord said, "As

Jonah was three days and three nights in the belly of the great fish, so will the Son of Man be three days and three nights in the heart of the earth" (Matthew 12:40). Jonah's "burial" in the belly of the great fish is symbolic of Christ's burial in the tomb of earth for three days, and the acceptable repentance of the Ninevites is reminiscent of our repentance throughout the Great Fast. Henceforth the Great Fast is the "Fast of fasts"!

Archdeacon Banoub Abdou's work, originally published in Arabic under the title "Knooz El Neima," is a vast compendium. This English translation by Saint Mary and Saint Demiana Convent in Georgia is not comprehensive, but only attempts to glean the highlights of his work for the Great Fast. A more comprehensive version of this book on the Great Fast, including the sermons, is currently under publication in three volumes. The translation is neither literal (rendering a rigid read), nor figurative (losing the intended meaning). However, it is a comfortable medium, carrying the meaning and spirit of his words and simultaneously an enjoyable read for the fluent English speaker. We would like to extend our deepest thanks to all who joyfully labored in the translation process, to bring this book to the light; may the Lord reward them with the heavenly in place of the earthly. All the credit goes to the Archdeacon's fluency in expressing himself, and any mistakes are to be blamed on us.

The purpose of this book is to aid the Coptic reader to understand why the church in her wisdom chose those specific passages to be read on each day during the Great and Holy Fast, and to aid every reader to dive deeper into the meanings within these select Biblical passages and muse over the beauty of God's word and its amazing linearity throughout the Holy Bible.

May the Lord use this work to enrich each Holy Bible reading and each reader during the Great and Holy Fast.

Metropolitan Youssef
Saint Mary and Saint Demiana Convent
January 14, 2023
Feast of Circumcision

UNIVERSAL THEME:

SALVATION THROUGH FAITH IN CHRIST THE MASTER'S RESURRECTION[1]

NINEVITES' FAST - MONDAY THE CALL TO REPENTANCE

(Calling sinners to repentance)

Linking the Readings:

All the readings of this day center on one theme: **Calling sinners to repentance**

The prophecy speaks of **God calling sinners to repent**, as He sent Jonah to the people of Nineveh (whose evil had risen to heaven) to call on them to repent.

The Vespers Gospel centers on the **Savior urging sinners to repent**, as He answered those who came to inform Him of the Galileans whose blood Pilate mingled with their sacrifices: "Unless you repent you will all likewise perish"; the Matins Gospel centers on **His mercy to sinners if they request forgiveness**, as shown by His saying that He gives good gifts to those who ask of Him; and the Liturgy Gospel centers on **cautioning the penitents against relapsing to sin**, as He spoke of the evil spirit that returned to the person who relapsed from his repentance bringing along seven other evil spirits.

The Pauline Epistle **urges penitents to offer their bodies unto holiness**, after having previously offered them to uncleanness and lawlessness; the Catholic Epistle centers on **the destruction of the impenitent**, describing them as "wandering stars for whom is reserved the blackness of darkness forever"; and the Acts reading speaks of **church**

[1] Resurrection from the dead, of which Jonah was a type.

expansion through the entry of penitent converts into the faith, as Peter baptized many, causing increased fellowship, "and the Lord added to the church daily those who were being saved."

PROPHECY

Prophecy Jonah 1:1–17

God calls sinners to repent: God called Jonah, the son of Amittai, to go to the people of Nineveh (whose wickedness had risen to Him) to call them to repent. Jonah instead fled from the face of the Lord to Tarshish on a ship. God sent a great storm against the ship causing its near submersion. When the mariners learned that the storm was because of Jonah, they reluctantly tossed him into the sea (heeding his advice) in an attempt to avoid drowning. God prepared a great fish to swallow Jonah, where he remained [in prayer] for three days and three nights.

PSALMS AND GOSPELS

Vespers Psalm Psalms 95:1–2

As sinners rush to repent, according to the Lord of Glory's call in the accompanying Gospel reading, this psalm shows their joy in receiving the forgiveness of their sins: "Oh come, let us sing to the Lord! Let us shout joyfully to the Rock of our salvation. Let us come before His presence with thanksgiving; let us shout joyfully to Him with psalms."

Vespers Gospel Luke 13:1–5

The Savior urges sinners to repent, as He told those who came to inform Him of the Galileans whose blood Pilate mingled with their sacrifices: "Unless you repent you will all likewise perish" (v. 5).

Matins Psalm Psalms 103:1, 8

The beginning of the psalm encourages sinners who tame their souls with fasting and prayer to bless God's Holy Name. The second part explains the reasons to bless His Name, which are that the Lord is compassionate and responds to their prayers, as shown in the Gospel reading. The psalm says, "Bless the Lord, O my soul; and all that is within me, bless His holy name! The Lord is merciful and gracious, slow to anger, and abounding in mercy."

Matins Gospel Matthew 7:6–12

The Gospel speaks of God's mercy to prayerful sinners who ask Him to forgive them and accept their repentance: "If you then, being evil, know how to give good gifts to your children, how much more will your Father who is in heaven give good things to those who ask Him" (v. 11).

Liturgy Psalm Psalms 130:3–4

Since on Judgment Day people will give an account for every idle word spoken, and anyone who relapses from repentance has a more evil end, the psalm speaks on behalf of sinners who have committed these sins and humbled themselves before God. It confesses that if He does not forgive them, they will perish, because He alone is the God of forgiveness, and they depend on His mercy: "If You, Lord, should mark iniquities, O Lord, who could stand? But there is forgiveness with You, that You may be feared."

Liturgy Gospel — Matthew 12:35–45

The Savior cautions penitents against the results of relapsing to sin, as He illustrated by the fate of the person who relapsed from repentance: ultimately, the evil spirit returns to him "and takes with him seven other spirits more wicked than himself... and the last state of that man is worse than the first" (v. 45).

EPISTLES

The Pauline Epistle — Romans 6:17–23

Urging penitents to offer their bodies unto holiness: Paul thanks God for the faithful, because although previously enslaved to sin, they obeyed, from their hearts, the form of doctrine delivered to them. "For just as you presented your members as slaves of uncleanness, and of lawlessness leading to more lawlessness, so now present your members as slaves of righteousness for holiness," revealing to them the result of either choice: "What fruit did you have then in the things of which you are now ashamed? For the end of those things is death. But now having been set free from sin, and having become slaves of God, you have your fruit to holiness, and the end, everlasting life" (vv. 19, 21–22).

The Catholic Epistle — Jude 1:1–13

Destruction of the impenitent: Jude charges the faithful to stand fast in the faith which was once for all delivered to the saints, warning against false teachers who creep in only to divert them from the

Lord's grace unto lewdness. He gives some examples: destruction of the Israelites who left Egypt yet did not believe; the angels who did not keep their proper domain; Sodom and Gomorrah; and those who perished in the rebellion of Korah—describing the destruction awaiting all those "wandering stars for whom is reserved the blackness of darkness forever" (v. 13).

The Acts Acts 2:38–47

Church expansion through the entry of converts into the faith: Peter the apostle charged his listeners to repent and be baptized in the name of the Lord Jesus for the remission of their sins. They joyfully accepted his words and were baptized, and that day three thousand persons joined the church, and they shared everything in common, being all with one accord: "And the Lord added to the church daily those who were being saved" (v. 47).

NINEVITES' FAST - TUESDAY
LISTENING TO THE GOSPEL

Linking the Readings:

All the readings of this day center on one theme: **Listening to the Gospel**

The prophecy speaks of **God listening to the repentance of sinners**, as He listened to the prayer of Jonah while he was in the belly of the great fish and ordered the fish to vomit him onto land, so that he may cry out to the people of Nineveh as He had ordered Jonah.

The Matins Gospel speaks of **God's patience with them** (perhaps they will hear His voice), as the landowner was patient with the unfruitful fig tree, giving it one more year; and the Liturgy Gospel focuses on the **Savior urging sinners to listen to the Gospel**, as He said that He had lit His lamp and placed it on a lamp stand so that all those who enter can see the light.

The Pauline Epistle speaks of the **importance of listening to the Gospel**, as the Apostle said that he preaches the Gospel to everyone, admonishing so that he "may present every man perfect in Christ Jesus"; the Catholic Epistle tells sinners they must **refrain from evil**; and the Acts reading **calls out to them to repent**, as shown by Paul the apostle explaining that God "commands all men everywhere to repent," and some of those who heard him believed.

PROPHECY

Prophecy Jonah 2:1–10

God listens to the repentance of sinners: This prophecy mentions the prayer that Jonah offered up to God from the belly of the great fish, in which he declared that he was surrounded by floods and covered over by billows and waves. When his soul grew faint, he remembered God's mercy and prayed to Him, promising to fulfill his vows. God listened to his repentance and commanded the great fish to vomit him onto dry land to call on the Ninevites.

PSALMS AND GOSPELS

Matins Psalm — Psalms 103:14–15, 9–10

The psalm's beginning hints at what comes in the Gospel reading regarding the landowner's patience for one more year on the unfruitful fig tree, and concludes by begging God not to deal with sinners according to their sins, but according to His mercy: "For He knows our frame; He remembers that we are dust. As for man, his days are like grass; as a flower of the field, so he flourishes. He will not always strive with us, nor will He keep His anger forever. He has not dealt with us according to our sins, nor punished us according to our iniquities."

Matins Gospel — Luke 13:6–9

This Gospel passage speaks of the Savior's patience with His people's sins (perhaps they will repent), as shown by the vinedresser asking the landowner of the unfruitful fig tree: "Sir, let it alone this year also, until I dig around it and fertilize it. And if it bears fruit, well. But if not, after that you can cut it down" (vv. 8–9).

Liturgy Psalm — Psalms 85:2–3

This psalm refers to what follows in the Gospel in that the Ninevites repented at Jonah's call to repent, and so God relented from the wrath of His anger towards them, as the Savior pointed out in the Gospel: "If then your whole body is full of light... the whole body will be full of light." And so, the psalm says, "You have forgiven the iniquity of Your people; You have covered all their sin. You have taken away all Your wrath; You have turned from the fierceness of Your anger."

Liturgy Gospel Luke 11:29–36

The Savior urges sinners to obey [the light of] the Gospel, which is set as a lamp shining before them: "If then your whole body is full of light, having no part dark, the whole body will be full of light, as when the bright shining of a lamp gives you light" (v. 36).

EPISTLES

The Pauline Epistle Colossians 1:21–29

Importance of listening to the Gospel: Paul reveals to believers that the Savior reconciles us in the body of His flesh through His death, only if they continue in the faith and do not move away from the hope of the Gospel, for which he is a minister, showing that the purpose of the call of the Gospel is "that we may present every man perfect in Christ Jesus" (v. 28).

The Catholic Epistle 1 Peter 4:3–11

Refraining from evil: Peter begins to address the sinners, urging them to refrain from evil: "For we have spent enough of our past lifetime in doing the will of the Gentiles—when we walked in lewdness, lusts..." Then he alerts them that, "the end of all things is at hand; therefore be serious and watchful in your prayers," and commands them: "If anyone speaks, let him speak as the oracles of God. If anyone ministers, let him do it as with the ability which God supplies" (vv. 3, 7, 11).

The Acts Acts 17:30–34

The call to repentance: This passage relays part of Paul's address to the Athenians at Areopagus: "Truly, these times of ignorance God overlooked, but now commands all men everywhere to repent," further clarifying to them that the Almighty has appointed a day in which He will judge the world with righteousness "by the Man whom He has ordained. He has given assurance of this to all by raising Him from the dead." Although some of the listeners mocked him when he mentioned the resurrection from the dead, others believed his words (vv. 30, 31).

NINEVITES' FAST - WEDNESDAY
FORGIVING THE PENITENTS

Linking the Readings:

All the readings of this day center on one theme: **Forgiving the penitents**

The prophecy speaks of **God accepting the repentance of sinners**, as He accepted the people of Nineveh when they repented at the call of Jonah.

The Matins Gospel speaks of **God's compassion on them**, as He promised to give rest to all those who are weary and heavy laden, if they come to Him; and the Liturgy Gospel speaks of **the Savior forgiving their sins**, as He fed the multitudes with the seven loaves (satiation being symbolic of the forgiveness of sins) and telling the Pharisees who asked Him for a sign that He will not give them any sign, but the sign of Jonah the Prophet.

The Pauline Epistle speaks of **saving the penitents by grace**, as the Apostle told the believers that they were saved by grace through faith; the Catholic Epistle urges them **not to love the world**, as the apostle commanded; and the Acts reading orders **not to overburden them**, as James the apostle judged in speaking of those returning to God from the Gentiles.

PROPHECY

Prophecy Jonah 3:1–4:11

God accepts penitents: This prophecy shows that after the great fish vomited Jonah the prophet onto land, he obeyed God's command and began to call to the people of Nineveh, warning them that their city will be overthrown after forty days. They believed, called a fast, and put on sackcloth; as a result, God relented from the evil He intended to do to them. God's mercy to them saddened Jonah, so God sent an unexpected plant to give him shade. Then it was struck by a worm and withered, which also saddened Jonah, so the Lord told him: "You have had pity on the plant for which you have not labored... And should I not pity Nineveh, that great city?" (vv. 4:10–11).

PSALMS AND GOSPELS

Matins Psalm — Psalms 103:13, 12

The start of the psalm refers to God's compassion on sinners by revealing His Gospel message to them and ends with the promise to give them rest, as mentioned in the Gospel passage that He will give rest to those who come to Him. The psalm says, "As a father pities his children, so the Lord pities those who fear Him. As far as the east is from the west, so far has He removed our transgressions from us."

Matins Gospel — Matthew 11:25–30

This passage speaks of the Savior's compassion on sinners who turn to Him: "Come to Me, all you who labor and are heavy laden, and I will give you rest" (v. 28).

Liturgy Psalm — Psalms 32:1, 5

The start of the psalm foreshadows the Gospel reading on feeding the multitude.[2] Then, speaking for the penitent sinners, the psalm

---

[2] The multitude who were satisfied by the seven loaves and few fish (a symbol of the forgiveness of sins).

confesses the Lord's forgiveness of their sins: "Blessed is he whose transgression is forgiven, whose sin is covered. I said, 'I will confess my transgressions to the Lord,' and You forgave the iniquity of my sin."

Liturgy Gospel — Matthew 15:32–16:4

This passage speaks of the Savior forgiving the sins of the penitents, as shown by satisfying the multitude with the seven loaves and the fish (symbolic of the forgiveness of sins [through the Eucharistic bread]). Afterwards, He tells the Pharisees who considered themselves satisfied: "A wicked and adulterous generation seeks after a sign, and no sign shall be given to it except the sign of the prophet Jonah" (v. 4).

EPISTLES

The Pauline Epistle — Ephesians 2:1–22

Salvation of penitents by grace: The apostle recounts that we were previously dead through sin (being by nature children of wrath) until God revived us in Christ Jesus and by [His] grace saved us through faith. He shows that we were created in Christ Jesus for good works, and charges us, having been brought near to Christ the Master, not to live as we have before, strangers and foreigners, "but fellow citizens with the saints and members of the household of God" (v. 19).

The Catholic Epistle — 1 John 2:12–17

Charging them not to love the world: The apostle cheers believers (young and old) for their victory over evil, clarifying to them that true knowledge of God is in keeping His commandments and loving the brethren. Then he charges them: "Do not love the world or the things in the world," revealing this mystery, "If anyone loves the world, the love of the Father is not in him" (v. 15).

The Acts — Acts 15:12–20

Not overburdening the penitents: In resolving the dispute that arose between the faithful over circumcision, and after listening to Paul and Barnabas, James passes this decree: "Therefore I judge that we should not trouble those from among the Gentiles who are turning to God, but that we write to them to abstain from things polluted by idols, from sexual immorality, from things strangled, and from blood" (vv. 19–20).

NINEVITES' FEAST
SALVATION THROUGH FAITH
(Faith in Christ the Master's Resurrection)

Linking the Readings:

All the readings of this day center on one theme: **Salvation through faith in the Resurrection of Christ the Master**

The Matins Gospel speaks of **His aid to those who believe in His ability to forgive their sins**, as He reminded the disciples (who had forgotten to take bread with them into the boat) of His aid to them on two previous occasions (symbolic of forgiving their sins); and the Liturgy Gospel speaks of **His authority to resurrect Himself from the dead**, as He verified this in telling the Jews[3], "Destroy this temple, and in three days I will raise it up," meaning the temple of His body.

The Pauline Epistle speaks of the **salvation of those who believe in His Resurrection**, as the Apostle states that whoever believes in His Resurrection will be saved; the Catholic Epistle speaks of their **salvation through baptism**, considering it symbolic of the Resurrection; and the Acts reading speaks of the **blessings of His Resurrection**, as Peter the apostle declared in his address to the Jews who were astonished at his healing of the crippled man.

PSALMS AND GOSPELS

Matins Psalm — Psalms 30:10–11

The second part of this psalm shows the gladness of sinners in God's forgiveness of their iniquities, which points to the Gospel

[3] Who requested a sign from Him to validate His authority to expel the merchants from the temple.

reading. There, the Savior reminds His disciples of His aid to them on two previous occasions in which He satiated them with few loaves—symbolic of the forgiveness of sins. With the tongue of these sinners, the first part of the psalm confesses this Divine aid: "Hear, O Lord, and have mercy on me; Lord, be my helper! You have turned for me my mourning into dancing; You have put off my sackcloth and clothed me with gladness."

Matins Gospel — Mark 8:10–21

This passage speaks of the Savior's help to those who believe in His power to forgive sins, as He reminded the disciples that He had fed them twice from the bread (symbolic of [the Eucharistic bread] the means by which sins are forgiven): "Why do you reason because you have no bread? Do you not yet perceive nor understand?" (v. 17).

Liturgy Psalm — Psalms 118:5, 18

The psalm's beginning hints at the events concerning Jonah's prayer to God from the belly of the great fish who heard him and ordered it to vomit him out (through which Jonah was a type of Christ the Master who told the Jews in the Gospel passage, "Destroy this temple, and in three days I will raise it up" —meaning the temple of His body (John 2:19)). The psalm continues, indicating the trial Jonah underwent from which he was saved—again symbolic of Christ—and says, "I called on the Lord in distress; the Lord answered me and set me in a broad place. The Lord has chastened me severely, but He has not given me over to death."

Liturgy Gospel — John 2:12–25

This passage speaks of the Savior's authority to resurrect Himself, by Himself, as He told the Jews who requested a sign from Him to validate His authority to expel the merchants from the temple: "Destroy this temple, and in three days I will raise it up," meaning the temple of His body (v. 19).

EPISTLES

The Pauline Epistle Romans 10:4–18

Salvation of those who believe in His Resurrection: The first part of this passage shows the difference between the righteousness of the law and the righteousness of faith in Christ the Master. Then, Paul charges the faithful to believe in the Savior's Resurrection from the dead by saying: "If you confess with your mouth the Lord Jesus and believe in your heart that God has raised Him from the dead, you will be saved." He further details that those who believe in Him will not be put to shame (whether Jews or Greeks) and that the Word will reach the Gentiles, who will accept it (v. 9).

The Catholic Epistle 1 Peter 3:17–22

Salvation through baptism (symbolic): The apostle shows believers that it is better if they suffer for doing good than to suffer for doing evil, giving them Christ the Master as an example, who, being just, suffered for the unjust: "There is also an antitype which now saves us—baptism (not the removal of the filth of the flesh, but the answer of a good conscience toward God), through the resurrection of Jesus Christ" (v. 21).

The Acts Acts 3:22–26

Blessings of His Resurrection: As Peter the apostle addresses the Jews regarding the healed crippled man, he shows that faith in the name of Christ the Master is what strengthened this man, and that Moses preceded and foretold of the Savior, through whose name this man was healed. He further preached to them to believe in Jesus and His Resurrection, to receive His blessings, and to turn away from their iniquities: "To you first, God, having raised up His Servant Jesus, sent Him to bless you, in turning away every one of you from your iniquities" (v. 26).

UNIVERSAL THEME:
PREPARING TO FAST

LEAVE-TAKING SATURDAY
THE NEED TO REPENT

Linking the Readings:

All the readings of this day center on one theme: **The need to repent**

In the Vespers Gospel, the Savior exhorts believers on the need to **forgive those who sin against them**; in the Matins Gospel on **keeping vigil (watchfulness) against sin**; and in the Liturgy Gospel on **repentance**.

In the Pauline Epistle, Paul encourages them to sorrow—**sorrow leading to repentance**; in the Catholic Epistle to **rejoice over their salvation**; and in the Acts reading to **suffer for the sake of Christ**.

PSALMS AND GOSPELS

Vespers Psalm — Psalms 17:1–2

Speaking for believers who forgive those who sin against them (as instructed in the Gospel passage), the psalm beckons God to answer their prayers: "Hear a just cause, O Lord, attend to my cry; give ear to my prayer which is not from deceitful lips. Let my vindication come from Your presence; let Your eyes look on the things that are upright."

Vespers Gospel — Luke 17:3–6

In this passage, the Savior exhorts believers to forgive those who sin against them, saying: "And if he sins against you seven times in a day, and seven times in a day returns to you, saying, 'I repent', you shall forgive him" (v. 4).

Matins Psalm Psalms 119:49, 52

Speaking for watchful believers who are cautious against sinning (as the Savior urges in the Gospel passage), this psalm seeks the Savior's promise to them, on which they have hope: "Remember the word to Your servant, upon which You have caused me to hope. I remembered Your judgments of old, O Lord, and have comforted myself."

Matins Gospel Mark 13:33–37

In this passage, the Savior exhorts believers to keep vigil, to be watchful against sin, saying, "Watch therefore, for you do not know when the master of the house is coming" (v. 35).

Liturgy Psalm Psalms 95:1–2

Speaking for believers who repented, and rejoiced in being rescued from the condemnation of non-penitents, this psalm praises God and encourages them to continue confessing their sins: "Oh come, let us sing to the Lord! Let us shout joyfully to the Rock of our salvation. Let us come before His presence with thanksgiving; let us shout joyfully to Him with psalms."

Liturgy Gospel Luke 13:1–5

In this passage, the Savior exhorts believers to repent: "Unless you repent you will all likewise perish" (v. 5).

EPISTLES

The Pauline Epistle 2 Corinthians 6:14–7:16

Sorrow leading to repentance: The apostle charges believers to flee from the fellowship and defilement of idol worship (because their souls are temples of the living God), commanding them to cleanse themselves from the filthiness of the flesh and spirit. He expresses the extent of the great comfort he experienced in his tribulations when he learned from Titus about their desire, mourning, and zeal for himself. Although he saddened them with his letter, yet he says, "Now I rejoice, not that you were made sorry, but that your sorrow led to repentance... For godly sorrow produces repentance leading to salvation, not to be regretted; but the sorrow of the world produces death" (vv. 9–10).

The Catholic Epistle 1 Peter 1:1–12

Believers' joy over the salvation of their souls: The apostle blesses God for "an inheritance incorruptible and undefiled and that does not fade away, reserved in heaven," showing that, although they might be temporarily grieved now through various trials, they will rejoice with inexpressible joy and glory, "receiving the end of your faith—the salvation of your souls" (vv. 4, 9).

The Acts Acts 21:1–14

Suffering for the sake of Christ: This passage shows how the disciples tried, in vain, to prevent Paul from going to Jerusalem and how Agabus prophesied, concerning Paul, by binding himself with Paul's belt. To this, Paul responded: "I am ready not only to be bound, but also to die at Jerusalem for the name of the Lord Jesus" (v. 13).

LEAVE-TAKING SUNDAY
CORNERSTONES OF WORSHIP

Linking the Readings:

All the readings of this day center on one theme: **The cornerstones of worship**

In the Vespers Gospel, the Lord of Glory exhorts believers to **forgive those who wrong them**, so that they likewise are forgiven; in the Matins Gospel, on **their duty to worship Him**; in the Liturgy Gospel, on **observing the three cornerstones of worship**: charity (almsgiving), prayer, and fasting; and the Evening Gospel promises to **give them the Holy Spirit**, which He pours out on them in answer to their prayers.

In the Pauline Epistle, Paul calls their attention to the necessity of **caring for the service**, listing the internal and external hardships he suffered for the service; the Catholic Epistle speaks of **confirming their faith by good works**; and the Acts reading **warns them** to "keep themselves from things offered to idols, from blood, from things strangled, and from sexual immorality."

PSALMS AND GOSPELS

Vespers Psalm — Psalm 46:10

In the psalm, God exhorts believers to have faith in Him (as shown in the accompanying gospel passage), showing them that He will be exalted in the nations by answering the requests of the steadfast in the faith: "Be still, and know that I am God; I will be exalted among the nations, I will be exalted in the earth!"

Vespers Gospel Mark 11:22–26

In this passage, the Savior [tells believers to "have faith in God" and] exhorts them to forgive those who wrong them (before standing up to pray), so that their heavenly Father would also forgive them: "And whenever you stand praying, if you have anything against anyone, forgive him, that your Father in heaven may also forgive you your trespasses" (v. 25).

Matins Psalm Psalms 100:2–3

This psalm urges believers who forgive those who sin against them (as shown in the accompanying gospel passage) to serve God joyfully, not considering this forgiveness as a favor granted, but as their duty as sheep of His pasture: "Serve the Lord with gladness; come before His presence with singing. We are His people and the sheep of His pasture."

Matins Gospel Luke 17:3–10

This passage speaks of believers' duty to worship God, as the Savior commanded those who forgive others: "So likewise you, when you have done all those things which you are commanded, say, 'We are unprofitable servants. We have done what was our duty to do'" (v. 10).

Liturgy Psalm Psalms 2:11, 10

This psalm shows that even people of high standing, like kings or judges, need to fulfill the cornerstones of worship (those mentioned in the accompanying gospel passage) with fear and trembling: "Serve the Lord with fear, and rejoice with trembling. Now therefore, be wise, O kings; be instructed, you judges of the earth."

Liturgy Gospel Matthew 6:1–18

In this passage, the Savior encourages believers to observe the three cornerstones of worship: charity (almsgiving), prayer, and fasting: "When you do a charitable deed, do not sound a trumpet before you ... when you pray, you shall not be like the hypocrites... when you fast, do not be like the hypocrites" (vv. 2, 5, 16).

Evening Psalm Psalm 17:14

This psalm points to the believers who are filled with His Holy Spirit and His gifts, who give of the overflow to their children (as He said In the accompanying Gospel that though they are wicked when compared with His Almighty Holiness they know how to give good gifts to their children): "And whose belly You fill with Your hidden treasure. They are satisfied with children [swine flesh], and leave the rest of their possession for their babes."

Evening Gospel Luke 11:1–13

This passage speaks of the gift of the Holy Spirit that God pours out on believers in answer to their prayers: "If you then, being evil, know how to give good gifts to your children, how much more will your heavenly Father give the Holy Spirit to those who ask Him!" (v. 13)

EPISTLES

The Pauline Epistle 2 Corinthians 11:16–28

Believers' concern for the service: The apostle reveals to the Corinthians that, according to the law, he lags in nothing when compared with their esteemed false prophets. He shows that he endured much more than them in the service of Christ the Master; he endured various trials for the sake of this service. After listing these external hardships, he mentions the internal ones: "Besides the other things, what comes upon me daily: my deep concern for all the churches" (v. 28).

The Catholic Epistle 2 Peter 1:1–11

Confirming their faith through good works: The apostle establishes believers in the hope of God's abounding grace, charging them to add to their faith various good works (which he lists), concluding: "Therefore, brethren, be even more diligent to make your call and election sure [The Coptic text adds: "by good works"], for if you do these things you will never stumble" (v. 10).

The Acts Acts 21:15–26

Some restrictions: This passage mentions Paul reaching Jerusalem and describing to the disciples all that God had done among the Gentiles through his ministry. Then comes James' decision regarding those who believe, instructing them to "keep themselves from things offered to idols, from blood, from things strangled, and from sexual immorality" (v. 25).

NINEVITES' FAST: SALVATION THROUGH FAITH IN CHRIST'S RESURRECTION

	PROPHECY	**PSALMS & GOSPELS**			***EPISTLES***		
DAY	***Jonah***	**Vespers**	**Matins**	**Liturgy**	***Pauline***	***Catholicon***	***Acts***
MONDAY: THE CALL TO REPENTANCE	*God calling sinners to repent*	The Savior urges sinners to repent	The Savior mercy to sinners if they request forgiveness	He cautions penitents against relapsing to sin	*Urging penitents to offer their bodies unto holiness*	*Destruction of the impenitent*	*Church expansion through repentance*
TUESDAY: LISTENING TO THE GOSPEL	*God listens to the repentance of sinners*		God's patience with people's sins	He urges them to obey the Gospel	*The importance of listening to the Gospel*	*Refraining from evil*	*The call to repentance*
WEDNESDAY: FORGIVING THE PENITENTS	*God accepts penitents*		His compassion on the penitent	He forgives their sins	*Saving the penitents by grace*	*Charging them not to love the world*	*Not overburdening the penitents*
NINEVITES' **FEAST:** SALVATION THROUGH FAITH			The Savior's ability to forgive their sins	His authority to resurrect Himself	*Saving those who believe in His Resurrection*	*Their salvation through baptism*	*The blessings of His Resurrection*

LEAVE-TAKING DAYS: PREPARING TO FAST

	PSALMS & GOSPELS				***EPISTLES***		
DAY	**Vespers**	**Matins**	**Liturgy**	**Evening**	***Pauline***	***Catholicon***	***Acts***
SATURDAY: THE NEED TO REPENT	Believers need to forgive those who sin against them	Believers need to keep vigil (watchfulness) against sin	The Savior exhorts believers to repent		*Sorrow leading to repentance*	*Joy over saving their souls*	*Suffering for the sake of Christ*
SUNDAY: THE CORNERSTONES OF WORSHIP	Believers need to forgive those who wrong them	Believers have a duty to worship God	Observing the 3 cornerstones of worship: charity, prayer, and fasting	The Holy Spirit's gifts are poured out on believers in answer to their prayers	*Believers' concern for the service*	*Confirming their faith through good works*	*Some restrictions*

PART I: FEATURES OF THE STRUGGLE

UNIVERSAL THEME:
Preparing for the Struggle

FIRST WEEK – MONDAY
FORSAKING EVIL

Linking the Readings:

All the readings of this day center on one theme: **Forsaking evil**

The first prophecy speaks of **God manifesting Himself to those who cry out to Him from sin**, as He appeared to Moses in the burning bush; and the second prophecy speaks of Him **admonishing His people to abandon sin**, as He admonished the Israelites on the mouth of His prophet Isaiah.

The Matins Gospel speaks of God's **wrath against sinners**, as was His wrath against the Pharisees for their blasphemy; and the Liturgy Gospel speaks of how **He gives life to those who forsake sin**.

The Pauline Epistle speaks of **the judgment of sinners**; the Catholic Epistle explains how **their condemnation will be without mercy**; and the Acts reading speaks of **opening the door of faith** to them, as God opened it to the Gentiles on the hands of Saints Paul and Barnabas.

PROPHECIES

First Prophecy — Exodus 2:23–3:5

God manifests Himself to those who cry out to Him from sin: This prophecy speaks of Israel's groaning and crying out to God over their slavery in Egypt—symbolic of slavery to sin. After mentioning God hearing them (remembering His covenant with Abraham, Isaac, and Jacob), it shows God manifesting Himself in the burning bush which burns with fire, but is not consumed. He calls out to Moses from within saying: "Take your sandals off your feet, for the place where you stand is holy ground"[4] (v. 5).

Old Testament Type: The bush is not consumed
New Testament Antitype:

1) Unity of the Divinity with the Humanity taken from Saint Mary without mixing, mingling, or change
2) The One Nature of Christ the Master
3) Saint Mary conceives and remains a virgin

Second Prophecy — Isaiah 1:2–18

Admonishing His people to abandon sin: In this passage, God laments the sins of the Israelites, announcing His rejection of their offerings, and His hatred of their New Moons and feasts, then He addresses them saying: "Your hands are full of blood. Wash yourselves, make yourselves clean; put away the evil of your doings from before My eyes. Cease to do evil" (vv. 15–16).

[4] The Burning Bush is located in the Monastery of Saint Catherine in Sinai. Behind the altar there is a small church consisting of one room named after Saint Mary. Reportedly, it has been erected on the spot of the burning bush from which God spoke to Moses. Every Saturday (except Bright Saturday), the monks pray in it barefoot, out of respect for the divine words spoken to Moses.

PSALMS AND GOSPELS

Matins Psalm — Psalms 6:1–2

Seeing God's anger toward the Pharisees for their evils (as comes in the accompanying gospel passage), the psalm speaks for the believers, entreating God to heal them from the illness of sin: "O Lord, do not rebuke me in Your anger, nor chasten me in Your hot displeasure. Have mercy on me, O Lord, for I am weak; O Lord, heal me, for my bones are troubled."

Matins Gospel — Matthew 12:24–34

This passage speaks of God's wrath upon sinners as shown by the Savior's address to the Pharisees who accused Him of exorcizing the demon by Beelzebub: "Brood of vipers! How can you, being evil, speak good things?" (v. 34)

Liturgy Psalm — Psalm 22:26

This psalm relates to three points made by the Savior in the accompanying gospel passage: extoling humility; His saying, "No one who works a miracle in My name can soon afterward speak evil of Me" (Mark 9:39); and to the eternal life awaiting those who forsake the causes of sin. "The poor shall eat and be satisfied; those who seek Him will praise the Lord. Let your heart live forever."

Liturgy Gospel — Mark 9:33–50

This passage speaks of the Savior giving life to those who forsake the causes of sin, as He said to His disciples, "If your hand causes you to sin, cut it off. It is better for you to enter into life maimed, rather than having two hands, to go to hell, into the fire that shall never be quenched" (v. 43).

EPISTLES

The Pauline Epistle — Romans 1:26–2:7

Judgment of sinners: In this epistle, Paul rebukes sinners, "Filled with all unrighteousness, sexual immorality, wickedness, covetousness, maliciousness; full of envy, murder, strife, deceit, evil-mindedness; they are whisperers... who, knowing the righteous judgment of God, that those who practice such things are deserving of death, not only do the same but also approve of those who practice them." Then he warns them: "And do you think this, O man, you who judge those practicing such things, and doing the same, that you will escape the judgment of God? Or do you despise the riches of His goodness, forbearance, and longsuffering... But in accordance with your hardness and your impenitent heart you are treasuring up for yourself wrath in the day of wrath and revelation of the righteous judgment of God" (vv. 1:29, 32; 2:3–5).

The Catholic Epistle — James 2:1–13

Their condemnation is without mercy: The apostle speaks of the sin of partiality, showing that one who is partial transgresses the law, and will be judged without mercy: "For judgment is without mercy to the one who has shown no mercy" (v. 13).

The Acts — Acts 14:19–28

Opening the door of faith to them: This passage speaks of Paul and Barnabas' successful mission, and "[Having] gathered the church together, they reported all that God had done with them, and that He had opened the door of faith to the Gentiles," which signifies that the door of faith is open to sinners (who are labeled as Gentiles) if they obey the voice of the Gospel (v. 27).

FIRST WEEK – TUESDAY
CLINGING ONTO GOOD

Linking the Readings:

All the readings of this day center on one theme: **The believers' need to cling to good**

The first prophecy speaks of **guiding the Gentiles to God's law**, as Isaiah prophesied; and the second prophecy speaks of **God blessing them** as He blessed Judah and Israel.

The Matins Gospel **calls them to repent**, as the Lord Jesus frankly declares that He "did not come to call the righteous, but sinners, to repentance"; and the Liturgy Gospel speaks of the Savior's **mercy to penitent sinners** because of the forces opposing their repentance.

The Pauline Epistle speaks of **the riches of His glory** in calling sinners to become His people after having been Gentiles; the Catholic Epistle **exhorts them to do good;** and the Acts reading speaks of **enduring pain for Christ's sake**, as the Apostles endured from the Jews.

PROPHECIES

First Prophecy Isaiah 1:19–2:3

Guiding the Gentiles to God's law: The evangelical prophet shows "how the faithful city has become a harlot" (meaning the house of Israel), how its silver has become dross, its wine mixed with water, and its princes rebellious (who love bribes and seek rewards), not defending the fatherless and ignoring the cause of the widow. He concludes that God will purify her dross: "Zion shall be redeemed with justice, and her penitents with righteousness." Then, he prophesies of the reign of Christ's kingdom and laws: "Now it shall come to pass in the latter days that the mountain of the Lord's house shall be established on the top of the mountains... and all nations shall flow to it... For out of Zion shall go forth the law, and the word of the Lord from Jerusalem" (vv. 1:21, 27; 2:1–3).

Second Prophecy | Zechariah 8:7–13

God blessing them: In this prophecy, the Lord of Hosts speaks on the tongue of His prophet Zechariah: "But now I will not treat the remnant of this people as in the former days... For the seed shall be prosperous, the vine shall give its fruit, the ground shall give her increase, and the heavens shall give their dew... Just as you were a curse among the nations, O house of Judah and house of Israel, so I will save you, and you shall be a blessing. Do not fear, let your hands be strong" (vv. 11–13).

PSALMS AND GOSPELS

Matins Psalm | Psalms 23:1, 3

The start of this psalm refers to the accompanying gospel passage, which shows the coming of the Savior as His people's shepherd to call sinners to repentance, and then the psalm points to His response to John's disciples' question: "The Lord is my shepherd; I shall not want. He restores my soul; He leads me in the paths of righteousness."

Matins Gospel | Matthew 9:10–15

This passage speaks of the Savior's call for sinners to repent, as He told the Pharisees who derided Him for eating with tax collectors and sinners: "For I did not come to call the righteous, but sinners, to repentance" (v. 13).

Liturgy Psalm Psalms 25:16–17

This psalm points to the parable of the faithful steward that comes in the accompanying gospel passage, and with the tongue of the penitents ([the faithful servant and the penitent sinner] who are exposed to resistance and sorrows for the sake of their repentance) the psalm begs for God's mercy, saying: "Turn Yourself to me, and have mercy on me, for I am desolate and afflicted. The troubles of my heart have enlarged."

Liturgy Gospel Luke 12:41–50

This passage speaks of the Savior's mercy on penitent sinners against forces opposing them because of their repentance, saying: "I came to send fire on the earth, and how I wish it were already kindled," that is, as there is no salvation except through the fire of tribulations, I am eager to kindle it (v. 49).

EPISTLES

The Pauline Epistle Romans 9:15–29

Calling Gentiles to repentance: The apostle reveals that God shows mercy to the merciful, and compassion on the compassionate, and in this there is absolutely no injustice: "What if God, wanting to show His wrath and to make His power known, endured with much longsuffering the vessels of wrath prepared for destruction, and that He might make known the riches of His glory on the vessels of mercy, which He had prepared beforehand for glory, even us whom He called, not of the Jews only, but also of the Gentiles? As He says also in Hosea: 'I will call them My people, who were not My people, and her beloved, who was not beloved.'" Next, the apostle witnesses to the honesty of His call, as Isaiah says of Israel: "Though the number of the children of Israel be as the sand of the sea, the remnant will be saved. For He will finish the work and cut it short in righteousness" (vv. 22–28).

The Catholic Epistle 1 Peter 4:3–11

Admonishing them to do good: If the Pauline Epistle discusses God calling the Gentiles to be His people, then this epistle advises them of the need to break off from evil and begin doing good. Here, the apostle urges them further: "For we have spent enough of our past lifetime in doing the will of the Gentiles—when we walked in lewdness, lusts, drunkenness, revelries, drinking parties, and abominable idolatries." He continues: "But the end of all things is at hand; therefore be serious and watchful in your prayers. And above all things have fervent love for one another, for love will cover a multitude of sins" (vv. 3, 7–8).

The Acts Acts 5:34–42

Enduring pain for Christ's sake: This passage speaks of the faithful suffering pain for the sake of Christ, as shown by the following incident: being warned by Gamaliel not to harm the disciples, the Jews "agreed with him, and when they had called for the apostles and beaten them, they commanded that they should not speak in the name of Jesus, and let them go. So they departed from the presence of the council, rejoicing that they were counted worthy to suffer shame for His name" (vv. 40–41).

FIRST WEEK – WEDNESDAY
LOVING OTHERS

Linking the Readings:

All the readings of this day center on one theme: **Loving others**

The first prophecy exhorts believers to **fear the Lord** in all their dealings, as Isaiah charged the house of Jacob; and the second prophecy speaks of **God's blessings to those who fear Him**, as Joel promised the people of God.

The Matins Gospel commissions believers to **love their enemies**, specifically, while the Liturgy Gospel speaks of **loving others**, generally, showing that their reward will be based on their deeds.

The Pauline Epistle speaks of **pleasing others**; the Catholic Epistle reveals that our **love for them must be practical**; and the Acts reading speaks of **loving the upright**, even if they are Gentiles, as Peter revealed to Cornelius.

PROPHECIES

First Prophecy — Isaiah 2:3–11

Believers fear the Lord in all their dealings: Isaiah shows that at the coming of Christ the Master's kingdom, many people will go to Zion—the source of the Law—and there the Lord will judge justly. Then, he charges the house of Jacob to fear God in all their dealings with others: "O house of Jacob, come and let us walk in the light of the Lord," showing that they were rejected because of their evil, that "the haughtiness of men shall be bowed down, and the Lord alone shall be exalted in that day" (vv. 5, 11).

Second Prophecy Joel 2:12–27

God's blessings to those who fear Him: Joel the prophet charges God's people to return to Him, calling out to them: "Turn to Me with all your heart, with fasting, with weeping, and with mourning. So rend your heart, and not your garments." He mentions that the Lord is zealous for His land and pities His people: "Behold, I will send you grain and new wine and oil, and you will be satisfied by them; I will no longer make you a reproach among the nations." He then gladdens them by saying: "So I will restore to you the years that the swarming locust has eaten... You shall eat in plenty and be satisfied... My people shall never be put to shame" (vv. 12–13, 19, 25–27).

PSALMS AND GOSPELS

Matins Psalm Psalms 25:6–7

Speaking for believers who have fulfilled the Savior's commandments mentioned in the accompanying Gospel (loving their enemies, doing good to those who hate them, and blessing those who curse them), the psalm supplicates God to forgive their sins, as they forgave others: "Remember, O Lord, Your tender mercies and Your loving-kindnesses, for they are from of old. Do not remember the sins of my youth, nor my transgressions."

Matins Gospel Luke 6:24–34

This passage shows the Savior exhorting the believers to love their enemies: "Love your enemies, do good to those who hate you, bless those who curse you" (vv. 27–28).

Liturgy Psalm Psalms 25:20, 16

Speaking for believers who have fulfilled the Savior's commandments in the accompanying Gospel (loving others, doing good, and lending, in imitation of their heavenly Father), this psalm supplicates God to have mercy on them as they had mercy on others: "Keep my soul, and deliver me; let me not be ashamed, for I put my trust in You. Turn Yourself to me, and have mercy on me."

Liturgy Gospel Luke 6:35–38

This passage shows that the Savior is just to those who love others, rewarding them according to their works: "For with the same measure that you use, it will be measured back to you" (v. 38).

EPISTLES

The Pauline Epistle Romans 14:19–15:7

Pleasing others: The apostle commands believers to pursue things that make for peace and the things by which one may edify another. Then he says, "We then who are strong ought to bear with the scruples of the weak, and not to please ourselves. Let each of us please his neighbor for his good, leading to edification" (vv. 15:1–2).

The Catholic Epistle 2 Peter 1:4–11

Our love for them must be practical: The apostle commands believers: "Add to your faith virtue, to virtue knowledge, to knowledge self-control, to self-control perseverance, to perseverance godliness, to godliness brotherly kindness, and to brotherly kindness love," revealing that love must be active: "Therefore, brethren, be even more diligent to make your call and election sure [the Coptic text adds "by good works"]" (vv. 5–7, 10).

The Acts Acts 10:9–20

Loving the upright, even if they are Gentiles: This passage mentions Peter's vision, in which he saw a great sheet let down from heaven containing creeping things and birds of the air, and the first voice saying: "Rise, Peter; kill and eat," then the response based on his objection: "What God has cleansed you must not call common." Doubtless, this indicates the need to accept all the upright, even if they are Gentiles, as Peter revealed to Cornelius: "In every nation whoever fears Him and works righteousness is accepted by Him" (vv. 13, 15, 35).

FIRST WEEK – THURSDAY
SPIRITUAL GROWTH

Linking the Readings:

All the readings of this day center on one theme: **Spiritual growth**, that is, the believers' growth in the grace of the Gospel

The first prophecy speaks of **the Gospel's superiority over idols**, as Isaiah prophesied of this at the coming of Christ's kingdom; and the second prophecy speaks of **all nations turning to Him**, as the Gentiles turned to Jerusalem seeking God's face when Jerusalem's glory was restored.

The Matins Gospel speaks of **His authority over nature**, as clearly seen in the Savior's authority over the wind and sea; and the Liturgy Gospel speaks of the **growth of those who seek and obey the Gospel**—spiritual growth by divine power, just as plants sprout and grow by God's power.

The Pauline Epistle addresses how **believers need to walk in the seriousness of the Gospel**, as Paul charged the Corinthians; the Catholic Epistle speaks of **steadfastness in the Gospel**, as John the apostle commanded; and the Acts reading speaks of the **signs that follow those who evangelize**, as was seen with Philip.

PROPHECIES

First Prophecy — Isaiah 2:11–19

The Gospel's superiority over idols: In this prophecy, Isaiah reveals what will happen when Christ's kingdom arises: "The lofty looks of man shall be humbled, the haughtiness of men shall be bowed down, and the Lord alone shall be exalted in that day... But the idols He shall utterly abolish," illustrating the superiority of the Gospel over idolatrous worship (vv. 11, 18).

Second Prophecy Zechariah 8:18–23

All nations turn to Him: This prophecy shows that the mandated fasts will turn into joy, gladness, and cheerful feasts for the house of Judah. Then it clarifies that the Gentiles will turn to Jerusalem, seeking God's face when Jerusalem's glory is restored: "Many peoples and strong nations shall come to seek the Lord of hosts in Jerusalem, and to pray before the Lord... [Then] ten men from every language of the nations shall grasp the sleeve of a Jewish man, saying, 'Let us go with you, for we have heard that God is with you'" (vv. 22–23).

PSALMS AND GOSPELS

Matins Psalm Psalms 24:1–2

This psalm alludes to the accompanying gospel passage, where Christ the Master reveals His authority over nature: "The earth is the Lord's, and all its fullness, the world and those who dwell therein. For He has founded it upon the seas, and established it upon the waters."

Matins Gospel Luke 8:22–25

In this passage, the Savior displays His authority over nature, as the disciples remarked when they saw Him still the wind and save the boat: "Who can this be? For He commands even the winds and water, and they obey Him" (v. 25).

Liturgy Psalm Psalms 118:14, 18

Speaking for those who embrace the Gospel and obey it, this psalm confesses that God has enriched their spiritual growth and salvation (paralleling this spiritual growth with what comes in the accompanying gospel passage, which shows that God is the One who enriches crops—and not the farmer), and that Almighty God has allowed them to be chastened, yet has saved them: "The Lord is my strength and song, and He has become my salvation. The Lord has chastened me severely, but He has not given me over to death."

Liturgy Gospel Mark 4:21–29

This passage shows that God provides spiritual growth for those who receive and live by His Gospel—akin to the parable of the growth of the crop without the farmer's contribution. This is shown by the Savior's saying to His disciples: "For whoever has, to him more will be given; but whoever does not have, even what he has will be taken away from him," that is, whoever receives the word of life and lives by it grows spiritually in virtue, but the one who receives it and does not live by it forfeits its value (v. 25).

EPISTLES

The Pauline Epistle 1 Corinthians 4:16–5:9

Walking in the seriousness of the Gospel: In this epistle, Paul rebukes the Corinthians for accepting the sexually immoral person, commanding them to deliver him "to Satan for the destruction of the flesh that his spirit may be saved." Then, he instructs them to purge out the old leaven to be a new lump, saying: "Therefore let us keep the feast, not with old leaven, nor with the leaven of malice and wickedness, but with the unleavened bread of sincerity and truth" (vv. 5:5, 8).

The Catholic Epistle 1 John 1:8–2:11

Steadfastness in the Gospel: Here, the apostle clarifies that whoever claims to know Christ yet "does not keep His commandments, is a liar, and the truth is not in him." He continues: "He who says he abides in Him ought himself also to walk just as He walked," and gives an example: "He who loves his brother abides in the light, and there is no cause for stumbling in him" (vv. 2:4, 6, 10).

The Acts Acts 8:3–13

Signs that follow those who evangelize: This passage catalogues the great signs Philip had done, "For unclean spirits, crying with a loud voice, came out of many who were possessed; and many who were paralyzed and lame were healed." Then this passage shows that: "Simon himself also believed; and when he was baptized he continued with Philip, and was amazed, seeing the miracles and signs which were done" (vv. 7, 13).

FIRST WEEK – FRIDAY
RELIANCE ON GOD

Linking the Readings:

All the readings of this day center on one theme: **Reliance on God**—the need of the believers to rely on Him

The first prophecy speaks of **God's blessings to those who rely on Him**, as He promised the children of Israel if they obey Him; while the second prophecy speaks of **the entire lack that the wicked** will endure, as Isaiah promised Jerusalem and Judah in consequence to their grave evils.

The Matins Gospel speaks of Him **healing those who take refuge in Him from the illness of sin**, as the Lord Jesus healed the leper; and the Liturgy Gospel speaks of **His goodness to all who ask of Him**, as He promised, "Ask, and it will be given to you; seek, and you will find; knock, and it will be opened to you."

The Pauline Epistle speaks of **serving others from what we have been granted**; the Catholic Epistle speaks of **welcoming strangers**, as John the apostle praised Gaius for his hospitality to strangers; and the Acts reading speaks of **serving from what we have**, as Peter, with the gift of healing that he was granted, healed the man crippled from his mother's womb.

PROPHECIES

First Prophecy — Deuteronomy 6:3–7:26

God's blessings to the obedient: This prophecy speaks of God's blessings to those who abide by His commandments [and rely on Him], as He said to Israel: "Because you listen to these judgments, and keep and do them, that the Lord your God will keep with you the covenant and the mercy which He swore to your fathers. And He will love you and bless you and multiply you; He will also bless the fruit of your womb and the fruit of your land, your grain and your new wine and your oil, the increase of your cattle and the offspring of your flock... there shall not be a male or female barren among you or among your livestock. And the Lord will take away from you all sickness" (vv. 7:12–15).

Second Prophecy Isaiah 3:1–14

The entire lack of the wicked: This prophecy completes the previous meaning, showing that God plundered all from the wicked: "For behold, the Lord, the Lord of hosts, takes away from Jerusalem and from Judah the stock and the store, the whole supply of bread and the whole supply of water; the mighty man and the man of war, the judge and the prophet, and the diviner and the elder; the captain of fifty and the honorable man, the counselor and the skillful artisan, and the expert enchanter. I will give children to be their princes, and babes shall rule over them" (vv. 1–4).

PSALMS AND GOSPELS

Matins Psalm Psalms 30:1–2

Speaking on behalf of the leper in the accompanying gospel passage (symbolic of those leprous with sin), this psalm glorifies God for caring for and healing him: "I will extol You, O Lord, for You have lifted me up, and have not let my foes rejoice over me. O Lord my God, I cried out to You, and You healed me."

Matins Gospel Luke 5:12–16

This passage shows that the Savior heals the sins of sick believers who take refuge in Him, as He answered the leper who entreated Him saying: "'Lord, if You are willing, You can make me clean'... 'I am willing; be cleansed.' Immediately the leprosy left him" (vv. 12–13).

Liturgy Psalm Psalms 13:5–6

This psalm alludes to the Gospel passage which shows that God responds to the prayers of those who rely on Him, and so praises Him: "But I have trusted in Your mercy; my heart shall rejoice in Your salvation. I will sing to the Lord, because He has dealt bountifully with me."

Liturgy Gospel Luke 11:1–10

This passage shows God's goodness to all who ask of Him, as He advised His disciples after giving them the example of borrowing three loaves: "So I say to you, ask, and it will be given to you; seek, and you will find; knock, and it will be opened to you" (v. 9).

EPISTLES

The Pauline Epistle Romans 12:6–21

Serving others with their talents: In this passage, the apostle commands believers to serve each other with their various gifts, encouraging them to care for others: "Be kindly affectionate to one another with brotherly love... Do not set your mind on high things, but associate with the humble." He concludes his exhortation: "Do not be overcome by evil, but overcome evil with good" (vv. 10, 16, 21).

The Catholic Epistle 3 John 1:1–14[5]

Welcoming strangers: Here, the apostle praises the beloved Gaius for his kindly treatment of brethren and strangers: "We therefore ought to receive such, that we may become fellow workers for the truth." In blaming Diotrephes (who does not receive the brethren, but puts them out of the church), he addresses Gaius saying, "Do not imitate what is evil, but what is good. He who does good is of God, but he who does evil has not seen God" (vv. 8, 11).

The Acts Acts 2:42–3:9

Serving from what they have: This passage starts by showing how "all who believed were together, and had all things in common." Then it speaks of Peter and John healing the man lame from his mother's womb, to whom Peter said: "Silver and gold I do not have, but what I do have I give you: In the name of Jesus Christ of Nazareth, rise up and walk" (vv. 2:44; 3:6).

[5] This numbering differs in the Coptic text such that 1 John has 15 verses, while the English has only 14 verses; it is the same content of the entire epistle that is read here.

FIRST WEEK – SATURDAY
WALKING IN PERFECTION

Linking the Readings:

All the readings of this day center on one theme: **Walking in perfection**

The Matins Gospel speaks of some of **the Savior's laws to believers who are walking in perfection**; and the Liturgy Gospel speaks of **encouraging them to imitate His perfection**.

The Pauline Epistle speaks of the **importance of doing good**; the Catholic Epistle speaks of **being patient during temptations**; and the Acts reading speaks of believers' **exposure to trials for the word's sake,** as Paul was subjected to by the Jews.

PSALMS AND GOSPELS

Matins Psalm Psalms 119:57–58

This psalm alludes to the Savior's commandments to His people (that are mentioned in the accompanying gospel passage), and speaking for them, it entreats Him, begging mercy, and saying: "You are my portion, O Lord; I have said that I would keep Your words. I entreated Your favor with my whole heart; be merciful to me according to Your word."

Matins Gospel Matthew 5:25–37

This passage speaks of the Savior's commandments to His people: "Agree with your adversary quickly, while you are on the way with him... But I say to you that whoever looks at a woman to lust for her has already committed adultery with her in his heart... But I say to you, do not swear at all... But let your 'Yes' be 'Yes,' and your 'No', 'No'" (vv. 25, 28, 34, 37).

Liturgy Psalm — Psalms 5:1–2

Speaking for believers, this psalm confesses God's royalty and divinity (indicating His befitting perfection that is mentioned in the accompanying Gospel) and pleads with Him to answer their requests: "Give ear to my words, O Lord, consider my meditation. Give heed to the voice of my cry, my King and my God."

Liturgy Gospel — Matthew 5:38–48

This passage shows how the Savior encourages believers to imitate His perfection: "Therefore you shall be perfect, just as your Father in heaven is perfect" (v. 48).

EPISTLES

The Pauline Epistle — Romans 12:1–21

The importance of doing good: In this epistle, Paul commissions believers not to imitate this world, then he says: "But be transformed by the renewing of your mind, that you may prove what is that good and acceptable and perfect will of God." Then, he urges them to "abhor what is evil. Cling to what is good... [and]... Have regard for good things in the sight of all men" (vv. 2, 9, 17).

The Catholic Epistle James 1:1–12

Being patient during temptations: Here, James encourages believers to be patient and endure when they fall into various trials, and then reveals the reward for those who endure: "Blessed is the man who endures temptation; for when he has been approved, he will receive the crown of life which the Lord has promised to those who love Him" (v. 12).

The Acts Acts 21:27–39

Exposure to trials for the word's sake: This passage speaks of Paul being tried before the commander after the whole city became unsettled: "And all the city was disturbed; and the people ran together, seized Paul, and dragged him out of the temple; and immediately the doors were shut." They sought to kill him, but news of him reached the commander, who inquired into his case (v. 30).

FIRST WEEK – SUNDAY[6]
LEADING TO GOD'S KINGDOM

Linking the Readings:

All the readings of this day center on one theme: **Leading to God's Kingdom**—the Savior leading the believers to this kingdom

The Vespers Gospel speaks of the Savior **exhorting believers to pray**; the Matins Gospel speaks of Him **confirming those who keep His sayings**; the Liturgy Gospel speaks of the Savior **guiding them to His kingdom**; and the Evening Gospel speaks of **His commandments to them**.

The Pauline Epistle speaks of the need for the believers to **walk properly**; the Catholic Epistle speaks of them **accepting the word with meekness**; and the Acts reading speaks of them **calling on the Name of the Lord**, as Ananias also encouraged Paul to do.

PSALMS AND GOSPELS

Vespers Psalm — Psalms 17:1–2

This psalm alludes to the accompanying gospel passage in which the Lord said "ask, and it will be given to you; seek and you will find," and speaking for faithful believers (who walk in perfection), it cries out to Him and says: "Hear a just cause, O Lord, attend to my cry; give ear to my prayer which is not from deceitful lips. Let my vindication come from Your presence; let Your eyes look on the things that are upright."

---

[6] Since the readings of this preceding week (the weeks here culminate on Sunday) center on preparing for the struggle, it has been called "Preparation Week" since the time of Pope Demetrius the Vinedresser in the fourth century.

Vespers Gospel Matthew 6:34–7:12

This passage exhorts believers to pray, as the Savior directed His disciples: "Ask, and it will be given to you; seek, and you will find; knock, and it will be opened to you" (v. 7).

Matins Psalm Psalms 18:1–2

This psalm alludes to the accompanying gospel passage in which the Savior likened those who hear His sayings and keep them to one who built his house on the rock, and speaking for the believers who rely on Him: "I will love You, O Lord, my strength. The Lord is my rock and my fortress and my deliverer; my God, my strength, in whom I will trust."

Matins Gospel Matthew 7:22–29

In this passage, the Savior confirms those who keep His sayings: "Therefore whoever hears these sayings of Mine, and does them, I will liken him to a wise man who built his house on the rock" (v. 24).

Liturgy Psalm Psalms 25:1–2, 4–5

This psalm alludes to the accompanying gospel passage in which the Lord of Glory directs the believers' attention to seek first the kingdom of God and His righteousness, and to rely on Him: "To You, O Lord, I lift up my soul. O my God, I trust in You; let me not be ashamed; show me Your ways, O Lord; teach me Your paths. Lead me in Your truth."

Liturgy Gospel Matthew 6:19–33

This passage speaks of the Savior leading believers to the kingdom of God and His righteousness as He said to them: "But seek first the kingdom of God and His righteousness, and all these things shall be added to you" (v. 33).

Evening Psalm Psalms 48:10–11

This psalm alludes to the accompanying gospel passage in which the Savior establishes commandments for believers to follow, exhorting them to rejoice in them: "Your right hand is full of righteousness. Let Mount Zion rejoice, let the daughters of Judah be glad, because of Your judgments."

Evening Gospel Luke 6:27–38

In this passage, the Savior commands believers to love their enemies: "But love your enemies, do good, and lend, hoping for nothing in return" (v. 35).

EPISTLES

The Pauline Epistle Romans 13:1–14

Needing to walk properly: In this epistle, Paul charges believers to be subject to authorities, to love one another, and to walk properly as in the day. Summing up this behavior, he says, "But put on the Lord Jesus Christ, and make no provision for the flesh, to fulfill its lusts" (v. 14).

The Catholic Epistle James 1:13–21

Accepting the word with meekness: Here, James shows that a person is tempted when drawn away by desires, and that when desire conceives, it gives birth to sin. Then he commands believers: "Therefore lay aside all filthiness and overflow of wickedness, and receive with meekness the implanted word, which is able to save your souls" (v. 21).

The Acts Acts 21:40–22:16

Calling on the Name of the Lord: This passage shows Paul's defense before the commander in which he retells how he was called [to the faith], and what Ananias said to him after he regained his sight: "The God of our fathers has chosen you that you should know His will, and see the Just One, and hear the voice of His mouth. For you will be His witness to all men of what you have seen and heard. And now why are you waiting? Arise and be baptized, and wash away your sins, calling on the name of the Lord" (vv. 22:14–16).

WEEK 1: PREPARING FOR THE STRUGGLE

			PSALMS & GOSPELS		***EPISTLES***		
DAY	***PROPHECIES***		**Matins**	**Liturgy**	***Pauline***	***Catholicon***	***Acts***
MONDAY: FORSAKING EVIL	*1* ***Ex****: God is manifest to those crying out to Him from sin*	*2* ***Is****: God admonishes His people to leave sin*	God's wrath against sinners	God gives life to those who forsake sin	*Judgment of sinners*	*Their judgment is without mercy*	*Opening the door of faith to them*
TUESDAY: CLINGING ONTO GOOD	*1* ***Is****: Guiding the Gentiles to God's law*	*2* ***Zech****: His blessings to them*	Calling them to repentance	The Savior's mercy to penitent sinners	*The richness of His glory in calling Gentiles to repentance*	*Admonishing them to do good*	*Enduring pain for Christ's sake*
WEDNESDAY: LOVING OTHERS	*1* ***Is****: Believers fear the Lord in all their dealings*	*2* ***Joel****: God's blessings to those who fear Him*	Believers are commissioned to love their enemies, specifically	Loving others, for the reward will be based on their deeds	*Pleasing others*	*Our love for them must be practical*	*Loving the upright, even if they are Gentiles*
THURSDAY: SPIRITUAL GROWTH	*1* ***Is****: The Gospel's superiority over idols*	*2* ***Zech****: All nations turn to Him*	His authority over nature	Spiritual growth of those who seek and obey Him	*Walking in the seriousness of the Gospel*	*Steadfastness in living the Gospel*	*Signs of those who evangelize*
FRIDAY: RELIANCE ON GOD	*1* ***Deut****: His blessings to the obedient*	*2* ***Is****: The lack (want) of the wicked in everything*	Healing those who take refuge in Him from the illness of sin	His goodness to those who ask of Him	*Serving others with our gifts*	*Welcoming strangers*	*Serving from our possessions*
SATURDAY: WALKING IN PERFECTION			The Savior's commandments to His people	He encourages believers to imitate His perfection	*The importance of doing good*	*Being patient in temptations*	*Exposure to trials for the word's sake*
SUNDAY: LEADING BELIEVERS TO GOD'S KINGDOM	**Vespers Gospel** He exhorts believers to pray	**Matins Gospel** He confirms those who keep His sayings	**Liturgy Gospel** Leading believers to the kingdom of God	**Evening Gospel** Commanding believers to love their enemies	*Needing to walk properly*	*Accepting the word with meekness*	*Calling on His Name*

UNIVERSAL THEME:
NATURE OF THE STRUGGLE

SECOND WEEK – MONDAY
STRUGGLING TO PRAY

(Prayer as one cornerstone of struggle)

Linking the Readings:

All the readings of this day center on one theme: **The need to pray**—as a cornerstone of the struggle

The first prophecy speaks of **God answering the prayers of those who fear Him**, as He answered the cries of the Israelites in Egypt; and the second prophecy speaks of **Him rejecting the prayers of the wicked**, as He commanded the clouds not to rain on His vineyard, Israel, which produced wild grapes.

The Matins Gospel speaks of **God's mercy on those who pray to Him with faith**, as the Savior did for the father of the demon-possessed boy; and the Liturgy Gospel speaks of **offering prayers persistently, until they are answered**, as the widow did with the unjust judge.

The Pauline Epistle speaks of **God's wrath on those who forsake prayer**; the Catholic Epistle speaks of **their condemnation as a warning or an example to others**; and the Acts reading speaks of the **retribution on those who offer prayer unfaithfully**, as occurred with Ananias and Sapphira.

PROPHECIES

First Prophecy — Exodus 3:6–14

God answers the prayers of those who fear Him: This passage speaks of God calling out to Moses from the burning bush: "I have surely seen the oppression of My people who are in Egypt, and have heard their cry because of their taskmasters, for I know their sorrows. So I have come down to deliver them... Come now, therefore, and I will send you to Pharaoh that you may bring My people, the children of Israel, out of Egypt." Doubtless, this incident represents the believers' enslavement to Satan and sin, their cry to God for liberation, and His answer to them by sending His Son for their salvation (vv. 7–8, 10).

Second Prophecy — Isaiah 4:2–5:7

Rejecting the prayers of the wicked: Isaiah the prophet opens by indicating the coming of Christ the Master's kingdom (when the children of Israel's wickedness reaches its climax), then continues, revealing their pending punishment and God's rejection of their prayers, because He expected His vineyard (His people) "to bring forth good grapes, but it brought forth wild grapes." So, He says, "And now, please let Me tell you what I will do to My vineyard: I will take away its hedge, and it shall be burned; and break down its wall, and it shall be trampled down. I will lay it waste; it shall not be pruned or dug, but there shall come up briers and thorns. I will also command the clouds that they rain no rain on it" (vv. 5:2, 5–6).

PSALMS AND GOSPELS

Matins Psalm — Psalm 40:11

Speaking for the father of the demon-possessed boy from whom the disciples were unable to exorcise the demon (mentioned in the accompanying gospel passage), the psalm successfully entreats God's mercy: "Do not withhold Your tender mercies from me, O Lord; let Your lovingkindness and Your truth continually preserve me."

Matins Gospel — Mark 9:25–29

This passage speaks of the Savior's mercy on those who entreat Him with faith, asking for salvation from captivity to Satan, as did the demon-possessed boy's father. The Master's words to His disciples, after He exorcised the demon, confirm: "This kind can come out by nothing but prayer and fasting" (v. 29).

Liturgy Psalm — Psalms 29:1–2

This psalm urges believers to present God with the holy offertory unceasingly, and the sacrifices of praise (prayers) —unrelenting until they are answered—just as the widow did with the unjust judge in the accompanying gospel passage: "Bring to the Lord, ye sons of God, bring to the Lord young rams; bring to the Lord glory and honor. Bring to the Lord glory, due to his name."[7]

Liturgy Gospel — Luke 18:1–8

In this passage, the Savior urges believers to lift up their prayers to God persistently until they are answered, as the widow did with the

[7] Here the LXX version was used for accuracy.

unjust judge, and He says: "And shall God not avenge His own elect who cry out day and night to Him, though He bears long with them?" (v.7)

EPISTLES

The Pauline Epistle — Romans 1:18–25

God's wrath on those who forsake prayer: The apostle opens this passage by saying: "For the wrath of God is revealed from heaven against all ungodliness and unrighteousness of men," revealing the reason: "Because, although they knew God, they did not glorify Him as God, nor were thankful, but became futile in their thoughts, and their foolish hearts were darkened." He finishes by revealing what will become of them: "Therefore God also gave them up to uncleanness, in the lusts of their hearts, to dishonor their bodies among themselves" (vv. 18, 21, 24).

The Catholic Epistle — Jude 1:1–8

Their condemnation is a warning: In this passage, Jude commands believers to "contend earnestly for the faith which was once for all delivered to the saints. For certain men have crept in unnoticed, who long ago were marked out for this condemnation, ungodly men, who turn the grace of our God into lewdness and deny the only Lord God and our Lord Jesus Christ." He proceeds to reveal that even "the angels who did not keep their proper domain... He has reserved in everlasting chains under darkness for the judgment of the great day," and, "Sodom and Gomorrah... are set forth as an example, suffering the vengeance of eternal fire" (vv. 3–4, 6, 7).

The Acts Acts 4:36–5:11

Retribution for unfaithfulness in prayer: This passage shows the story of Ananias and Sapphira (his wife). When the devil filled their hearts, they sold the land and kept back part of the price, giving the rest to the apostles. Peter told them that they had not lied to men but to God, and as a result they speedily received their just recompense, falling dead, one after the other, and "great fear came upon all the church" (v. 11).

SECOND WEEK – TUESDAY
STRUGGLING TO CONTRIBUTE
(Charity: a cornerstone of the struggle)

Linking the Readings:

All the readings of this day center on one theme: **Being charitable**—as a cornerstone of the struggle

The first prophecy **reveals to the charitable that they will see God on Judgment Day**, as Job declared concerning himself to his friends; and the second prophecy reveals the **destruction of the greedy**, as Isaiah warned.

In the Matins Gospel, the Savior commands believers **not to worry about food and clothing** as do the Gentiles, but to be concerned with the Kingdom of God; and in the Liturgy Gospel, He exhorts them to **give from their possessions**, as He suggested to the rich youth.

In the Pauline Epistle, Paul appeals to them to **give liberally and cheerfully—coupled with humility**—as James says in the Catholic Epistle. And Peter reveals in his address in the Acts reading that **charity is the spirit of faith**, as he revealed to the Jews after healing the man lame from his mother's womb who sat begging for alms.

PROPHECIES

First Prophecy Job 19:1–26

The charitable will see God on Judgment Day: This passage mentions that righteous Job, who was "blameless and upright, and one who feared God and shunned evil," a wealthy man who had offered many sacrifices to God, took to recounting to his friends all that had befallen him during his hard times, yet finally Job understood and said: "For I know that my Redeemer lives, and He shall stand at last on the earth; and after my skin is destroyed, this I know, that in my flesh I shall see God" (vv. 1:1; 19:25–26).

Second Prophecy Isaiah 5:7–16

Destruction of the greedy: In this passage, the Divine Revelation calls down to Isaiah with woes, desolation, and great events: "Woe to those who join house to house; they add field to field, till there is no place," showing the punishment [to the greedy] in this life: "Truly, many houses shall be desolate, great and beautiful ones, without inhabitant," and revealing their end in the age to come: "Therefore Sheol has enlarged itself and opened its mouth beyond measure; their glory and their multitude and their pomp, and he who is jubilant, shall descend into it" (vv. 8–9, 14).

PSALMS AND GOSPELS

Matins Psalm Psalms 41:4, 13

This psalm alludes to the believers (mentioned in the accompanying gospel passage) who care about providing food and clothing for their bodies while leaving their souls in spiritual starvation—the illness of sin—and entreats God on their behalf to heal them, and then blesses Him for satisfying their souls and bodies: "I said, Lord, be merciful to me; heal my soul, for I have sinned against You. Blessed be the Lord God of Israel from everlasting to everlasting! Amen and Amen."

Matins Gospel Luke 12:22–31

In this passage, the Savior urges His people to seek first the Kingdom of God, and not food and drink: "And do not seek what you should eat or what you should drink... But seek the kingdom of God, and all these things shall be added to you" (vv. 29, 31).

Liturgy Psalm — Psalm 41:1

This psalm encourages the believers to give charity (in accordance with the Savior's word to the rich youth in the accompanying gospel passage), showing that charity saves from trouble: "Blessed is he who considers the poor; the Lord will deliver him in time of trouble."

Liturgy Gospel — Mark 10:17–27

In this passage, the Savior urges believers to give charity from their possessions, as He told the rich youth: "Go your way, sell whatever you have and give to the poor, and you will have treasure in heaven; and come, take up the cross, and follow Me" (v. 21).

EPISTLES

The Pauline Epistle — 2 Corinthians 9:6–15

Giving liberally and cheerfully: In this passage, the apostle declares, "He who sows sparingly will also reap sparingly, and he who sows bountifully will also reap bountifully," then clarifies, "God loves a cheerful giver." Finally, he shows the reward to the charitable: "Now may He who supplies seed to the sower, and bread for food, supply and multiply the seed you have sown and increase the fruits of your righteousness" (vv. 6–7, 10).

The Catholic Epistle James 1:1–12

Charity coupled with humility: In this epistle, James mentions that God "gives to all liberally and without reproach," then encourages the rich to be humble: "Let the lowly brother glory in his exaltation, but the rich in his humiliation, because as a flower of the field he will pass away" (vv. 5, 9–10).

The Acts Acts 4:13–22

Charity is the spirit of faith: This passage shows Peter and John proclaiming to the Jews about faith in Christ the Master and the Resurrection. This is subsequent to their charity to the man, lame from his mother's womb, who was laid by the gate called Beautiful asking for alms. When they healed him, the leaders of the people and the elders of Israel were disturbed concerning Peter and John and the conversion of many to their teachings. They asked them not to mention the name of Jesus, but the two disciples responded: "Whether it is right in the sight of God to listen to you more than to God, you judge. For we cannot but speak the things which we have seen and heard" (vv. 19–20).

SECOND WEEK – WEDNESDAY
STRUGGLING FAITHFULLY

Linking the Readings:

All the readings of this day center on one theme: **Struggling faithfully**, without hypocrisy

The first prophecy speaks of **God's support for the faithful**, as the priest of Midian invited Moses to eat because of his faithfulness; the second prophecy reveals **His punishment to the unfaithful**, as Isaiah warned; and the third prophecy reveals **His reward to the faithful**, as Malachi promised Christ's light shining on them.

In the Matins Gospel, the Savior commands them to **be faithful in fulfilling the precepts of His new commandments** that declare the need to reconcile with all adversaries before offering gifts to God. In the Liturgy Gospel, He gives to them His aid by **satisfying them with the nourishment of His Gospel**, as He fed the multitudes from the seven loaves and the fish.

In the Pauline Epistle, Paul reveals that **God's faithfulness to the faithful is equivalent to His faithfulness to others**; the Catholic Epistle points to **His reward to them—the Father and the Son being their share**; and the Acts reading points to **His retribution on the unfaithful**, as occurred to Ananias and Sapphira.

PROPHECIES

First Prophecy — Exodus 2:11–20

God's support for the faithful: This passage mentions Moses' faithfulness. While visiting his own countrymen, he killed the Egyptian who was beating one of them. The following day, in trying to reconcile between two of them, when the offender threatened to expose the incident with the Egyptian, Moses escaped. Finally, he rescued the daughters of the priest of Midian, who told his daughters at their return: "Why is it that you have left the man? Call him, that he may eat bread" (v. 20).

Second Prophecy Isaiah 5:17–25

His punishment of the unfaithful: In this prophecy, Divine Revelation calls out, "Woe to those who call evil good, and good evil... Woe to those who are wise in their own eyes... Who justify the wicked for a bribe, and take away justice from the righteous man"; and then reveals their punishment: "Therefore, as the fire devours the stubble, and the flame consumes the chaff, so their root will be as rottenness, and their blossom will ascend like dust; because they have rejected the law of the Lord of hosts, and despised the word of the Holy One of Israel" (vv. 20–23, 24).

Third Prophecy Malachi 1:6–4:6[8]

God's reward to the faithful: In this prophecy, Divine Revelation reveals how the children of Israel despised the name of God, since they offered on His altar the stolen, lame, and sick. He promises that He will make them contemptible and base because they have strayed from the way and offended many by [their hypocritical observance of] the law. Then, He calls them to return to Him and so He will return to them. He concludes His speech by telling the faithful among them about the coming of His kingdom. "But to you who fear My name the Sun of Righteousness shall arise with healing in His wings; and you shall go out and grow fat like stall-fed calves. You shall trample the wicked, for they shall be ashes under the soles of your feet on the day that I do this, 'Says the Lord of hosts'" (vv. 4:2–3).

[8] This prophecy was removed in the new edition to the Katameros, published 1953.

PSALMS AND GOSPELS

Matins Psalm — Psalms 18:17–18

This psalm alludes to the accompanying gospel passage that reveals the scribes and Pharisees' disobedience of the Mosaic Law while the Savior accepts the offerings of believers and admits them into His kingdom—if they faithfully fulfill the commands of His law, which peacefully reconcile all adversaries and therefore says: "For they were too strong for me. They confronted me in the day of my calamity, but the Lord was my support."

Matins Gospel — Matthew 5:17–24

In this passage, the Savior urges believers to be faithful to His law and obey His commandments, which can reconcile all adversaries: "Therefore if you bring your gift to the altar, and there remember that your brother has something against you, leave your gift there before the altar, and go your way. First be reconciled to your brother, and then come and offer your gift" (vv. 23–24).

Liturgy Psalm — Psalms 18:1–2

The start of this psalm shows the multitude's love for Jesus which leads them to trust Him and follow Him for three days (having nothing to eat, as shown in the accompanying gospel passage [of the feeding of the multitude]); then it shows His support for them by satisfying them with seven loaves and the fish—pointing to the nourishment of the Gospel: "I will love You, O Lord, my strength. The Lord is my rock and my fortress and my deliverer; my God, my strength, in whom I will trust."

Liturgy Gospel Matthew 15:32–38

This passage shows the Savior's support for the faithful of His people, by satisfying them with the nourishment of the Gospel, as He said to His disciples about the multitude: "I do not want to send them away hungry, lest they faint on the way." He satisfied them with the seven loaves and the fish, symbolic of the nourishment of the Gospel (v. 32).

EPISTLES

The Pauline Epistle Romans 3:1–18[9]

God's faithfulness to the faithful is equivalent to His faithfulness to others: In the start of the passage, the apostle shows the advantage of the Jews over the Gentiles: "Because to them were committed the oracles of God." He continues that, despite the unfaithfulness of some, God's faithfulness cannot be negated: "Indeed, let God be true but every man a liar." Then, he asks on the tongue of believers: "What then? Are we better than they?" and responds, "Not at all," supporting his words by the inspired words: "There is none righteous, no, not one" (vv. 2, 4, 9, 10).

The Catholic Epistle 2 John 1:8–13

His reward to them: John alerts believers: "Whoever transgresses and does not abide in the doctrine of Christ does not have God. He who abides in the doctrine of Christ has both the Father and the Son."

---

[9] [The author had this passage ending at verse 17, but the reading actually ends at verse 18.]

Then he warns them: "If anyone comes to you and does not bring this doctrine, do not receive him into your house nor greet him" (vv. 9–10).

The Acts Acts 5:3–11

Retribution on the unfaithful: This passage speaks of punishing the unfaithful, represented by what happened to Ananias and Sapphira (as explained on Monday of this week).

SECOND WEEK – THURSDAY
CREDO OF THE STRUGGLE

(Needing to obey the Gospel as the law)

Linking the Readings:

All the readings of this day center on one theme: **The credo of the struggle**—the Holy Bible needs to be obeyed as the guideline for the struggle

The first prophecy speaks of **God giving His laws to His people of old**; the second prophecy reveals **His threats to those who reject the credo**, as Isaiah warned the Israelites; and the third prophecy reveals **His inheritance to those who obey the credo**, as He had given the Promised Land to the children of Israel.

In the Matins Gospel, the Savior calls His people to **bear the yoke of the Gospel** to find rest for their souls; and in the Liturgy Gospel, He promises them **eternal life if they forsake all and follow Him**.

In the Pauline Epistle, Paul charges believers to **reject all who teach contrary to the Gospel**; in the Catholic Epistle, James commands them to **control their tongues while [the Word is] being taught**; and the Acts reading shows His **retribution on those who oppose the Word's preachers**, as occurred with Herod when he withstood Peter.

PROPHECIES

First Prophecy — Deuteronomy 5:15–22

God gives His laws to His people of old: In this prophecy, Moses speaks to the children of Israel, revealing to them that God gave him the law on the mountain[10] from the midst of the fire. Then, he mentions to them the famous Ten Commandments, concluding the conversation: "These words the Lord spoke to all your assembly, in the mountain from the midst of the fire, the cloud, and the thick darkness, with a loud voice; and He added no more. And He wrote them on two tablets of stone and gave them to me" (v. 22).

Second Prophecy Isaiah 6:1–12

His threats to those who reject the credo: Here, Isaiah describes the throne of the Lord of Hosts surrounded by the heavenly hosts. He mentions one seraph coming with a coal in his hand with which he touched Isaiah's lips, and thus Isaiah's iniquity was removed. Then, the Lord said to him: "Go, and tell this people: keep on hearing, but do not understand... Make the heart of this people dull, and their ears heavy, and shut their eyes... until the cities are laid waste and without inhabitant" (vv. 9–11).

Third Prophecy Joshua 2:1–6:27[11]

His inheritance to those who obey the credo: This prophecy takes up five whole chapters from the book of Joshua speaking of the children of Israel crossing the Jordan, the fall of Jericho into their hands (because the Ark of the Covenant was with them), and their entry into the Promised Land—symbolic of God's people entering Heavenly Jerusalem.

---

[10] Located at the apex of Mount Sinai (the mount on which Saint Catherine's Monastery in Sinai stands) is a church after the name of the Holy Trinity, which has reportedly been established on the spot on which God gave Moses the Ten Commandments.

[11] This prophecy was removed in the new edition of the Katameros.

PSALMS AND GOSPELS

Matins Psalm — Psalm 28:9

Speaking with the tongue of babes, to whom the Lord revealed His Gospel (hiding it from the wise and prudent, who are also heavy laden with sin), and whom He called to Himself to give rest, this psalm begs God to give them salvation, blessings, and exaltation: "Save Your people, and bless Your inheritance; shepherd them also, and bear them up forever."

Matins Gospel — Matthew 11:20–30

In this passage, the Savior calls those who are heavy laden with sin, to bear the yoke of His Gospel and find rest for their souls: "Come to Me, all you who labor and are heavy laden, and I will give you rest" (v. 28).

Liturgy Psalm — Psalms 48:10–11

The start of the psalm alludes to the just reward that the Savior gives to those who leave everything and follow Him (as comes in the accompanying gospel passage), and then He urges them to rejoice in the Gospel commandments—the ones to which the Savior directed the attention of the rich young man: "Your right hand is full of righteousness. Let Mount Zion rejoice, let the daughters of Judah be glad, because of Your judgments."

Liturgy Gospel — Matthew 19:16–30

This passage speaks of the life the Savior gives to those who forsake all and follow Him, as He said to His disciples: "And everyone who has left houses or brothers or sisters… for My name's sake, shall receive a hundredfold, and inherit eternal life" (v. 29).

EPISTLES

The Pauline Epistle — Romans 16:17–27

Rejecting all who teach contrary to the Gospel: In this epistle, Paul commands believers to avoid anyone who teaches anything other than the message of the Gospel: "Now I urge you, brethren, note those who cause divisions and offenses, contrary to the doctrine which you learned, and avoid them." Then, after sending some greetings to the brethren, he entreats God to confirm them in the Gospel: "Now to Him who is able to establish you according to my gospel and the preaching of Jesus Christ… be glory through Jesus Christ forever. Amen" (vv. 17, 25, 27).

The Catholic Epistle — James 3:1–12

Controlling the tongue while teaching: In this passage, James commands believers to control their tongues while [the Word is] being taught, so as not to offend anyone: "My brethren, let not many of you become teachers, knowing that we shall receive a stricter judgment. For we all stumble in many things." He proceeds to show that the tongue "is an unruly evil, full of deadly poison," continuing, "these things ought not to be so" (vv. 1–2, 8, 10).

The Acts — Acts 12:12–23

His retribution on those who oppose the Word's preachers: This passage shows the believers' shock at seeing Peter return to them (after the angel released him from the prison into which Herod the king had thrown him). Herod gave the order to kill the prison guards because Peter had escaped, then he arrayed himself in royal apparel and addressed the people from his throne, until they cried out, "'The voice of a god and not of a man!' Then immediately an angel of the Lord struck him, because he did not give glory to God" (vv. 22–23).

SECOND WEEK – FRIDAY
STEADFASTNESS IN STRUGGLE
(Confirming those who keep the Gospel)

Linking the Readings:

All the readings of this day center on one theme: **Steadfastness in the struggle**, the steadfastness of those who keep the credo of the struggle—the Holy Bible

The first prophecy speaks of **God's inheritance for those who cling to His commandments**, as He promised Israel with the Promised Land; the second prophecy speaks of their **victory over their enemies**, as David overcame Goliath; the third prophecy **assures them**, as Ahaz was assured against his adversaries; and the fourth prophecy speaks of **God's grace to them**, as Zophar the Naamathite revealed to Job.

In the Matins Gospel, the Savior **warns against teachings contrary to the Gospel**, as He warned against the teachings of the Pharisees; and in the Liturgy Gospel, He **empowers those keeping the Gospel** until they become solid, as the house built on the rock.

In the Pauline Epistle, Paul commands them to **stand firm in the grace of the Gospel**; in the Catholic Epistle, Peter encourages them to **endure its sufferings**; and the Acts reading urges them to **heed its restrictions**, as the apostles commanded the believers to keep themselves from "things offered to idols, from blood, from things strangled, and from sexual immorality."

PROPHECIES

First Prophecy — Deuteronomy 8:1–9:4

God's inheritance for those who cling to His commandments: At the start of this passage, God orders the children of Israel to keep His commandments to them, "that you may live and multiply, and go in and possess the land of which the Lord swore to your fathers," and describes the land to them: "A land of wheat and barley, of vines and fig trees and pomegranates, a land of olive oil and honey." Then He warns them against forgetting the Lord in their satiety with food: "Lest—when you have eaten and are full... your heart is lifted up, and you forget the Lord your God." Finally, He commands them concerning their enemies: "Do not think in your heart, after the Lord your God has cast them out before you, saying, 'Because of my righteousness the Lord has brought me in to possess this land'" (vv. 8:1, 8, 12, 14; 9:4).

Second Prophecy — 1 Samuel 17:16–54; 18:6–9

Victory over their enemies: This passage speaks of David's victory over Goliath (the Philistine giant who defied Israel for forty days), and that Saul took David that day and did not allow him to return to his home, and that the dancing maidens' song of his glory and honor sparked Saul's envy.

Third Prophecy — Isaiah 7:1–14

Assuring the believers: This prophecy shows how King Ahaz of Judah was terrified at the arrival of the forces of the king of Syria and the king of Israel who came to fight against Jerusalem, yet the Lord responded on the tongue of Isaiah the prophet: "Take heed, and be quiet; do not fear or be fainthearted for these two stubs of smoking firebrands… It shall not stand, nor shall it come to pass." Then, He comforted the king with the sign—the promise of the Messiah: "Behold, the virgin shall conceive and bear a Son, and shall call His name Immanuel" (vv. 4, 7, 14).

Fourth Prophecy Job 11:1–20

God's grace to them: In this passage, Zophar the Naamathite responds to Job's grievance against life, censuring him for justifying himself, and showing him that God's wisdom is unfathomable, then advises him: "If you would prepare your heart, and stretch out your hands toward Him; if iniquity were in your hand, and you put it far away, and would not let wickedness dwell in your tents; then surely you could lift up your face without spot; yes, you could be steadfast, and not fear… And you would be secure, because there is hope… You would also lie down, and no one would make you afraid" (vv. 13–15, 18–19).

PSALMS AND GOSPELS

Matins Psalm Psalms 116:7–8

Alluding to the accompanying gospel passage in which the Savior reminds His disciples that He fed them with bread twice, assures them, and warns them of the teachings of the Pharisees who contradict the Gospel, this psalm says, "Return to your rest, O my soul, for the Lord has dealt bountifully with you. For You have delivered my soul from death, my eyes from tears, and my feet from falling."

Matins Gospel Matthew 15:39–16:12

In this passage, the Savior warns His disciples of the teachings of the Pharisees who contradict the Gospel, as the evangelist says, "Then they understood that He did not tell them to beware of the leaven of bread, but of the doctrine of the Pharisees and Sadducees" (v. 12).

Liturgy Psalm Psalms 29:10–11

Alluding to the accompanying gospel passage in which the Savior commands that those who preach the Gospel must first keep it, then promises to establish them, until they become as the house built on the rock, this psalm says: "The Lord sits as King forever. The Lord will give strength to His people; the Lord will bless His people with peace."

Liturgy Gospel Luke 6:39–49

This passage shows that the Savior empowers those who obey His Gospel, as He said to His disciples: "Whoever comes to Me, and hears My sayings and does them, I will show you whom he is like: he is like a man building a house, who dug deep and laid the foundation on the rock. And when the flood arose, the stream beat vehemently against that house, and could not shake it, for it was founded on the rock" (vv. 47–48).

EPISTLES

The Pauline Epistle Hebrews 12:28–13:16

Standing firm in the grace of the Gospel: In the start of this epistle, Paul commands believers who have gained the Gospel's grace to cling to it, then he charges them to remember their rulers and imitate their faith, warns them of strange teachings, and commands them to remain steadfast in the grace of the Gospel: "Do not be carried about with various and strange doctrines. For it is good that the heart be established by grace, not with foods which have not profited those who have been occupied with them" (v. 9).

The Catholic Epistle 1 Peter 4:7–16

Enduring suffering for the Gospel: Here, Peter encourages believers not to be surprised by the fiery trial occurring among them (to try them), commanding them to rejoice for having shared in the sufferings of Christ the Master, so that they may rejoice at the revelation of His glory: "But let none of you suffer as a murderer, a thief, an evildoer, or as a busybody in other people's matters. Yet if anyone suffers as a Christian, let him not be ashamed, but let him glorify God in this matter" (vv. 15–16).

The Acts Acts 15:22–31

Heeding the restrictions of the Gospel: This passage shows that the apostles, priests, and the whole church were pleased to send Judas and Silas to Antioch with Paul and Barnabas, to inform them that: "It seemed good to the Holy Spirit, and to us, to lay upon you no greater burden than these necessary things: that you abstain from things offered to idols, from blood, from things strangled, and from sexual immorality. If you keep yourselves from these, you will do well" (vv. 28–29).

SECOND WEEK – SATURDAY
TRIALS OF THE STRUGGLE
(Difficulties in the Holy Life)

Linking the Readings:

All the readings of this day center on one theme: **Trials of the struggle**—the trials accompanying the holy life

In the Matins Gospel, the Savior **instructs believers to avoid causes of offenses**; and in the Liturgy Gospel, He **encourages them to enter through the narrow gate**, to endure the difficulties of the holy life until they gain salvation.

In the Pauline Epistle, Paul urges believers **not to judge or offend each other**; in the Catholic Epistle, James charges them **not to be only hearers of the word, but also doers**; and the Acts reading reveals that it is necessary to **suffer in order to spread the Word**, as Paul suffered from the Jews and was driven to the examination.

PSALMS AND GOSPELS

Matins Psalm — Psalms 25:7, 8, 11

Speaking for believers, who are instructed to avoid offenses in the accompanying gospel passage, this psalm confesses their many iniquities and pleads with God to forgive them: "According to Your mercy remember me, for Your goodness' sake, O Lord. Good and upright is the Lord. For Your name's sake, O Lord, pardon my iniquity, for it is great."

Matins Gospel | Mark 9:43–50

This passage shows that the Savior commands believers to avoid the causes of offenses, as He says: "If your eye causes you to sin, pluck it out. It is better for you to enter the kingdom of God with one eye, rather than having two eyes, to be cast into hell fire" (v. 47).

Liturgy Psalm | Psalms 118:19–20

This psalm points to the commands of the Gospel, which it calls the gate of righteousness (the narrow gate mentioned in the accompanying gospel passage) and encourages believers to enter it: "Open to me the gates of righteousness; I will go through them, and I will praise the Lord. This is the gate of the Lord, through which the righteous shall enter."

Liturgy Gospel | Matthew 7:13–21

This passage shows that the Savior gives life to all who enter through the narrow gate: "Narrow is the gate and difficult is the way which leads to life, and there are few who find it" (v. 14).

EPISTLES

The Pauline Epistle | Romans 14:1–18

Not judging or offending one another: In this epistle, Paul urges believers to accept those who are weak in faith without meddling into their affairs, and charges them not to judge or despise the brethren, then commands them: "Therefore let us not judge one another anymore, but rather resolve this, not to put a stumbling block or a cause to fall in our brother's way" (v. 13).

The Catholic Epistle James 1:22–27

Not to be only hearers of the word, but also doers: Here, James directs the believers to "be doers of the word, and not hearers only, deceiving yourselves... He who looks into the perfect law of liberty and continues in it, and is not a forgetful hearer but a doer of the work, this one will be blessed in what he does" (vv. 22, 25).

The Acts Acts 22:17–30

Suffering in order to spread the word: This passage shows that the Jews rioted against Paul when he told them that God told him to: "Depart, for I will send you far from here to the Gentiles... [and] ...the commander ordered him to be brought into the barracks, and said that he should be examined under scourging, so that he might know why they shouted so against him." Yet, he was saved from scourging when he proved that he was a Roman citizen, and was later presented (by the commander's order) before the chief priests and the council for examination (vv. 21, 24).

SECOND WEEK – SUNDAY
VICTORY OF THE STRUGGLE[12]

Linking the Readings:

All the readings of this day center on one theme: **Victory of the struggle**—the Savior's victory for true believers over Satan's temptations against them

The four gospels of this day mention the story of the devil tempting the Savior in the wilderness; in each, a passage highlights one of the meanings specific to this topic. In the Vespers Gospel, the Savior **urges tempted believers to repent of the sins that lead to temptations**. The three remaining Gospel readings each point to one of Satan's three temptations of the Savior: lust of the flesh, lust of the eyes, and pride of life, as John mentions (1 John 2:16). In the Matins Gospel, the Savior **preserves those who are tempted with the pride of life**. Satan said, "Throw yourself down from here," and He responded, "It has been said, 'You shall not tempt the Lord your God.'" The Liturgy Gospel speaks of **aiding those tempted by the lust of the eyes**. Satan said, "All these things I will give you if you will fall down and worship me," to which the Savior responded, "It is written, you shall worship the Lord your God." The Evening Gospel speaks of Him **rescuing those tempted by the lust of the flesh**. Satan said, "Command this stone to become bread," to which He responded, "Man shall not live by bread alone."

In the Pauline Epistle, Paul warns believers against **offending the brethren by the lust of the flesh** (eating and drinking); in the Catholic Epistle, James charges them against **offending the brethren by the lust of the eyes** (partiality to the rich); and the Acts reading points to the **pride of life** (represented by the difference of opinion between the Pharisees and Sadducees regarding Paul's address).

---

[12] This Sunday is known as Temptation Sunday, as all the Gospel readings display the story of the devil tempting the Savior.

PSALMS AND GOSPELS

Vespers Psalm Psalms 51:1, 9

Speaking for believers enticed by their sins, this psalm begs God to flood them with His mercy and erase all these sins (as the Savior urges them in the accompanying gospel passage, "Repent and believe in the Gospel"): "Have mercy upon me, O God, according to Your lovingkindness; according to the multitude of Your tender mercies blot out my transgressions, hide Your face from my sins, and blot out all my iniquities."

Vespers Gospel Mark 1:12–15

In this passage, the Savior urges tempted believers to repent of their sins that led them into temptation: "Repent and believe in the gospel" (v. 15).

Matins Psalm Psalm 57:1

Alluding to the accompanying gospel passage, in which Satan addressed Christ the Master: "If You are the Son of God, throw Yourself down from here. For it is written: 'He shall give His angels charge over you, to keep you,'" this psalm speaks for those enticed by the pride of life and begs God to have mercy on them, showing that they have relied on Him: "Be merciful to me, O God, be merciful to me! For my soul trusts in You; and in the shadow of Your wings I will make my refuge, until these calamities have passed by."

Matins Gospel — Luke 4:1–13

This passage speaks of the Savior preserving believers who rely on His care without testing Him, as He answered Satan: "It has been said, 'You shall not tempt the Lord your God'" (v. 12).

Liturgy Psalm — Psalms 27:8–10

Speaking for believers who are enticed by the lust of the eyes, this psalm pledges that their worship is to God alone, and not to riches (alluding to the accompanying gospel passage in which Satan asks the Savior to worship him, after showing Him all the kingdoms of the world). Then it begs God to bestow upon them His help: "Your face, Lord, I will seek. Do not hide Your face from me; You have been my help; do not leave me nor forsake me, O God of my salvation."

Liturgy Gospel — Matthew 4:1–11

This passage shows that Jesus helps believers enticed by the lust of the eyes, who direct their worship to Him alone, as He answered Satan: "Away with you, Satan! For it is written, 'You shall worship the Lord your God, and Him only you shall serve'" (v. 10).

Evening Psalm — Psalm 41:1

This psalm encourages believers to consider the poor and the needy, so that God may rescue them from the temptation of the lust of the flesh (this is what is meant by "in time of trouble"), alluding to the accompanying gospel passage in which Satan tempts the Savior with bread: "Blessed is he who considers the poor; the Lord will deliver him in time of trouble."

Evening Gospel — Luke 4:1–13

This passage shows that the Savior rescues believers enticed by the lust of the flesh, as He said to Satan, "It is written, 'Man shall not live by bread alone, but by every word of God'" (v. 4).

EPISTLES

The Pauline Epistle — Romans 14:19–15:7

Offenses related to the lust of the flesh: In this epistle, Paul warns believers not to offend others by the lust of the flesh: "It is good neither to eat meat nor drink wine nor do anything by which your brother stumbles or is offended or is made weak." Then he shows that the offense is not from faith: "But he who doubts is condemned if he eats, because he does not eat from faith; for whatever is not from faith is sin." Then he also calls for their unity of opinion: "Now may the God of patience and comfort grant you to be like-minded toward one another, according to Christ Jesus" (vv. 14:21, 23; 15:5).

The Catholic Epistle — James 2:1–13

Offenses related to lust of the eyes: Here, James charges believers not to esteem the rich and scorn the poor, showing that this is a sin: "If you show partiality, you commit sin, and are convicted by the law as transgressors" (v. 9).

The Acts — Acts 23:1–11

Offenses related to pride of life: This passage shows that a great dissension occurred between the Pharisees and the Sadducees in the Jewish council as a result of Paul's address, and his life was placed in danger, yet the Lord's words to him by night were: "Be of good cheer, Paul; for as you have testified for Me in Jerusalem, so you must also bear witness at Rome" (v. 11).

WEEK 2: NATURE OF THE STRUGGLE

			PSALMS & GOSPELS		*EPISTLES*		
DAY	***PROPHECIES***		**Matins**	**Liturgy**	***Pauline***	***Catholicon***	***Acts***
MONDAY: STRUGGLING TO PRAY	*1 **Ex**: God answers the prayers of those who fear Him*	*2 **Is**: He rejects the wicked's prayers*	God's mercy is on those who pray to Him with faith	Believers need to persist in their prayer	*God's wrath is on those who forsake prayer*	*They are condemned —a warning*	*Retribution for unfaithfulness in prayer*
TUESDAY: STRUGGLING TO CONTRIBUTE	*1 **Job**: The charitable will see God on Judgment Day*	*2 **Is**: The greedy are destroyed*	Believers seek first the Kingdom of God	Believers give from their possessions	*Give liberally and cheerfully*	*Charity is coupled with humility*	*Charity is the spirit of faith*
WEDNESDAY: STRUGGLING FAITHFULLY	*1 **Ex**: God supports the faithful*	*2 **Is**: He punishes the unfaithful*	Be faithful in fulfilling His commandments	He nourishes believers with His Gospel	*God is faithful*	*His reward to believers*	*His retribution on the unfaithful*
	*3 **Mal**: God's reward to the faithful*						
THURSDAY: CREDO OF THE STRUGGLE	*1 **Duet**: God gives His laws to His people of old*	*2 **Is**: He threatens those who reject the credo*	Bear the yoke of the Gospel	Eternal life for those who forsake all to follow Him	*Reject all who teach contrary to the Gospel*	*Control the tongue while teaching*	*His retribution on those who oppose its preachers*
	*3 **Josh**: His inheritance is to those who obey the credo*						
FRIDAY: BEING STEADFAST IN STRUGGLE	*1 **Deut**: God's inheritance for those who follow His commandments*	*2 **1 Samuel**: Victory over their enemies*	He warns against teachings contrary to the Gospel	He empowers those keeping the Gospel	*Standing firm in the grace of the Gospel*	*Enduring its sufferings*	*Heeding its restrictions*
	*3 **Is**: Assuring the believers*		*4 **Job**: God's grace to them*				
SATURDAY: TRIALS OF THE STRUGGLE			He commands believers to avoid the causes of offenses	He encourages them to enter through the narrow gate	*Not judging or offending one another*	*Not being only hearers of the word, but also doers*	*Suffering in order to spread the word*
SUNDAY: VICTORY OF THE STRUGGLE	**Vespers Gospel** He urges tempted believers to repent	**Matins Gospel** He preserves those tempted by pride of life	**Liturgy Gospel** He aids those tempted by the lust of the eyes	**Evening Gospel** He rescues those tempted by the lust of the flesh	*Do not offend others by lust of the flesh*	*Do not offend others through lust of the eyes by showing partiality*	*Do not cause dissension through the pride of life*

UNIVERSAL THEME:
PURITY OF THE STRUGGLE (REPENTANCE)

THIRD WEEK – MONDAY
PENITENT CONFESSION
(Repentance leading to confession)

Linking the Readings:

All the readings of this day center on one theme: **Penitent confession**—repentance leading to confession

The first prophecy **urges believers to confess their sins**, as Wisdom urged the naive, foolish, and scornful to return to God at His rebuke; and the second prophecy speaks of **the Savior reigning over them**, as Christ's kingdom did shine on those sitting in darkness.

In the Matins Gospel, the Savior **floods them with grace**, as the king flooded the servant of the ten minas; and the Liturgy Gospel **promises them remission of their sins, if they confess them**.

In the Pauline Epistle, Paul urges **the brethren to be reconciled and to separate themselves from the evil person**; in the Catholic Epistle, Peter alerts them that **the end of their faith must be the salvation of their souls**; and the Acts reading reveals that they will be **exposed to the persecutions** accompanying those living a godly life, as Paul faced in Berea.

PROPHECIES

First Prophecy — Proverbs 1:20–33

Urging believers to confess their sins: In this passage, Wisdom urges believers [the naïve, the foolish, and the scornful] to repent: "How long, you simple ones, will you love simplicity? For scorners delight in their scorning, and fools hate knowledge. Turn at my rebuke." Then it warns the believers of what would become of them if they refuse to repent: "When your terror comes like a storm, and your destruction comes like a whirlwind, when distress and anguish come upon you. Then they will call on me, but I will not answer; they will seek me diligently, but they will not find me. Because they hated knowledge and did not choose the fear of the Lord" (vv. 22–23, 27–29).

Second Prophecy — Isaiah 8:13–9:7

The Savior reigning over them: In this passage, Isaiah begins by consoling those who hallow the Lord of Hosts and fear Him, saying on their behalf: "And I will wait on the Lord, who hides His face from the house of Jacob; and I will hope in Him. Here am I and the children whom the Lord has given me! We are for signs and wonders in Israel." Then, in the second part of the passage, he records the tragedies that will befall those who worship other gods: "They will pass through it hard pressed and hungry... they will be enraged and curse their king and their God... Then they will look to the earth, and see trouble and darkness, gloom of anguish; and they will be driven into darkness." Finally, in the third part, he speaks of Christ's kingdom shining on those who fear Him [those who had been sitting in darkness], and their joy with this kingdom and the birth of its Master: "The people who walked in darkness have seen a great light; those who dwelt in the land of the shadow of death, upon them a light has shined. You have multiplied the nation and increased its joy... For unto us a Child is born, unto us a Son is given; and the government will be upon His shoulder. And His name will be called Wonderful, Counselor, Mighty God, Everlasting Father, Prince of Peace" (vv. 8:17–18, 21–22; 9:2–3, 6).

PSALMS AND GOSPELS

Matins Psalm — Psalms 32:1–2

[According to the Master's command,] this psalm blesses the believers who confess their transgressions (for the Lord to forgive them) and clearly points to the accompanying gospel passage in which the Savior says that "to everyone who has will be given," saying, "Blessed is he whose transgression is forgiven, whose sin is covered. Blessed is the man to whom the Lord does not impute iniquity."

Matins Gospel — Luke 19:11–28

This passage speaks of the grace the Savior gives to those who confess their iniquities, as He said in the parable of the minas, in contrast to the servant who made no profit [not confessing his shortcomings]: "Take the mina from him, and give it to him who has ten minas... For I say to you, that to everyone who has will be given" (vv. 24, 26).

Liturgy Psalm — Psalm 32:5

Alluding to the accompanying gospel passage in which the Savior speaks about those who confess their sins (saying, "If then your whole body is full light"), and of His forgiveness of them (saying, "the whole *body* will be full of light"), the psalm states: "I acknowledged my sin to You, and my iniquity I have not hidden. I said, 'I will confess my transgressions to the Lord,' and You forgave the iniquity of my sin."

Liturgy Gospel Luke 11:33–36

This passage speaks of the Savior's forgiveness of those who confess their iniquities, as He said: "If then your whole body is full of light, having no part dark, the whole *body* will be full of light, as when the bright shining of a lamp gives you light" (v. 36).

EPISTLES

The Pauline Epistle 1 Corinthians 5:9–6:5

Urging the brethren to be reconciled: The apostle charges believers to avoid sinners and separate themselves from the evil person; then he exhorts them not to sue each other, but to pursue reconciliation: "Is it so, that there is not a wise man among you, not even one, who will be able to judge between his brethren?" (v. 6:5).

The Catholic Epistle 1 Peter 1:3–12

Directing them to salvation: In this epistle, Peter thanks God who "has begotten us again to a living hope through the resurrection of Jesus Christ from the dead, to an inheritance incorruptible and undefiled and that does not fade away." Then he alerts believers that the end of their faith must be the salvation of their souls, and shows that this salvation is not a new issue, but one which the prophets have foretold (vv. 3–4).

The Acts Acts 17:10–14

Exposure to persecutions: This passage speaks of the persecutions that those living a godly life will face, as Paul experienced in Berea (the brethren sent him there with his companion Silas after he had been persecuted in Thessalonica): "But when the Jews from Thessalonica learned that the word of God was preached by Paul at Berea, they came there also and stirred up the crowds" (v. 13).

THIRD WEEK – TUESDAY
THE RIGHTEOUSNESS OF REPENTANCE
(Repentance justifies the believers)

Linking the Readings:

All the readings of this day center on one theme: **The righteousness of repentance**—repentance justifies the believers

The first prophecy speaks of the **enlightenment of the penitents**, as the Sage revealed in the Proverbs; the second prophecy **warns them against arrogance**, so as not to be [subject to wrath] as Assyria; and the third prophecy speaks of **shunning treachery**, lest they are destroyed as was Achan.

In the Matins Gospel, the Savior incites them to the **need to reconcile disputes**; while the Liturgy Gospel **promises to free those who abide in His words.**

In the Pauline Epistle, Paul reveals that they are **justified by faith and works, [not works alone]**; in the Catholic Epistle, John charges them with **the love of the brethren**; and the Acts reading points to their **exposure to dangers** (among the necessities of the holy life) as Paul warned the men ready to set sail of the impending dangers.

PROPHECIES

First Prophecy — Proverbs 2:1–15

Enlightenment of the penitents: In this passage, Solomon the Sage directs the attention of believers to the impact of the Gospel on the souls: "My son, if you receive my words, and treasure my commands within you... Then you will understand the fear of the Lord, and find the knowledge of God." Then he shows that their enlightenment is based on this: "Then you will understand righteousness and justice, equity and every good path" (vv. 1, 5, 9).

Second Prophecy Isaiah 10:12–21

Warning them against arrogance: This prophecy shows God's anger is inflamed against oppressors (such as Assyria) who boast: "By the strength of my hand I have done it, and by my wisdom, for I am prudent." Therefore, He first ridicules them by saying: "Shall the ax boast itself against him who chops with it? Or shall the saw exalt itself against him who saws with it?" Then He pours out on them His full wrath: "Therefore the Lord, the Lord of hosts, will send leanness among his fat ones; and under his glory He will kindle a burning like the burning of a fire... And it will consume the glory of his forest and of his fruitful field, both soul and body" (vv. 13, 15, 16, 18).

Third Prophecy Joshua 7:1–26[13]

Shunning treachery: This passage shows that the children of Israel were defeated at Ai by the hands of the Amorites, so Joshua complained to God, who responded that it was due to the sin of Israel, as "they have also transgressed My covenant which I commanded them. For they have even taken some of the accursed things, and have both stolen and deceived." Then it shows how Achan confessed his theft: "When I saw among the spoils a beautiful Babylonian garment, two hundred shekels of silver, and a wedge of gold weighing fifty shekels, I coveted them and took them," and the result of his treachery: his being stoned and burned along with his sons, daughters, livestock, and what he had stolen (vv. 11, 21).

[13] This prophecy was removed in the new edition to the Katameros, published 1953.

PSALMS AND GOSPELS

Matins Psalm — Psalm 32:10

Alluding to the accompanying gospel passage, the start of this psalm refers to the prison into which anyone who does not reconcile with his brother is thrown (by the judge's orders), and then shows the reward for those who rely on God: "Many sorrows shall be to the wicked; but he who trusts in the Lord, mercy shall surround him."

Matins Gospel — Luke 12:54–59

In this passage, the Savior urges penitents to reconcile with their disputants, revealing the consequence to those who do not reconcile: "I tell you, you shall not depart from there till you have paid the very last mite" (v. 59).

Liturgy Psalm — Psalms 32:2–3

This psalm blesses the righteous man to whom God does not count sin, which is a sign indicating that the truth has set him free, as mentioned in the accompanying gospel passage. Then it shows that whoever is 'silent' (one who does not confess his sin), his bones will grow old (his conscience will bother him): "Blessed is the man to whom the Lord does not impute iniquity, and in whose spirit there is no deceit. When I kept silent, my bones grew old."

Liturgy Gospel — John 8:31–39

This passage shows that the Savior grants freedom to the penitent, as He told the Jews who believed: "If you abide in My word, you are My disciples indeed. And you shall know the truth, and the truth shall make you free" (v. 31–32).

EPISTLES

The Pauline Epistle Romans 4:1–8

Justification of the penitents through faith: The apostle begins by indicating the correctness of the notion that justification is through faith, which means faith with works, but not works alone; therefore, he mentions the condition of Abraham, of whom it was said: "Abraham believed God, and it was accounted to him for righteousness. Now to him who works, the wages are not counted as grace but as debt" (vv. 3–4).

The Catholic Epistle 1 John 2:1–11

Loving the brethren: Here, John charges believers not to sin, and to keep the commandments of the Savior, alerting them that "the darkness is passing away, and the true light is already shining." Then he exhorts them to love the brethren: "He who says he is in the light, and hates his brother, is in darkness until now... and does not know where he is going, because the darkness has blinded his eyes" (vv. 8–11).

The Acts Acts 27:9–12

Exposure to dangers: In this passage, Paul warns the men ready to set sail of the impending dangers: "Men, I perceive that this voyage will end with disaster and much loss, not only of the cargo and ship, but also our lives." In this saying is a sure sign of the dangers the true believers will be exposed to (among the necessities of the holy life) on their voyage from this turbulent world to their original state in heaven (v. 10).

THIRD WEEK – WEDNESDAY
TRIALS OF REPENTANCE
(Temptations accompanying the godly life)

Linking the Readings:

All the readings of this day center on one theme: **The trials of repentance**—temptations accompanying the godly life

The first prophecy speaks of **God's promise to rescue the tempted**, as He promised the children of Israel in Egypt; the second prophecy speaks of **His consolations to them**, as He promised Zion; the third prophecy **warns them against injustice**, as Isaiah warned Israel; and the fourth prophecy speaks of **their future hope in Him**, as Job placed his hope after death in God.

The Matins Gospel speaks of **the word of salvation's protection of the believers**, as the birds of heaven nest under the tree, which originally was simply a mustard seed; while the Liturgy Gospel speaks of **overcoming the wars of Satan through His mercy to them**, as He overcame the diabolic wars.

In the Pauline Epistle, Paul charges them to be **steadfast during temptations**; in the Catholic Epistle, Peter charges them to **avoid the wicked**; and the Acts reading speaks of **people honoring the believers**, as the natives honored Paul and his companions.

PROPHECIES

First Prophecy — Exodus 4:19–6:13

God's promise of rescuing the tempted: This prophecy mentions that Moses returned to Egypt to deliver God's message (on his mouth) for Pharaoh to release the children of Israel from Egypt. Pharaoh censured Moses and Aaron his brother for this and increased persecution against the children of Israel. They cried to Moses, who cried on their behalf to God, who renewed His covenant with them: "I will bring you out from under the burdens of the Egyptians, I will rescue you from their bondage... And I will bring you into the land which I swore to give to Abraham, Isaac, and Jacob" (vv. 6:6, 8).

Second Prophecy Joel 2:21–26

His consolations to them: In this prophecy, God comforts Zion and promises her present and future blessings: "Be glad then, you children of Zion, and rejoice in the Lord your God; for He has given you the former rain faithfully... I will restore to you the years that the swarming locust has eaten... You shall eat in plenty and be satisfied... and My people shall never be put to shame" (vv. 23–26).

Third Prophecy Isaiah 9:9–10:4

Warning them against injustice: In this passage, God pours out His wrath full strength on Israel for their arrogance, pride, and hypocrisy; then He calls down woes, destruction, and grand events on "those who decree unrighteous decrees, who write misfortune, which they have prescribed to rob the needy of justice, and to take what is right from the poor of My people, that widows may be their prey, and that they may rob the fatherless" (vv. 10:1–2).

Fourth Prophecy Job 12–14

Their future hope in Him: In this passage, Job responds to his friends' censure, confesses God's might, and takes to rebuking them. He places his trust and hope in God, asking God Almighty to reveal his sin and His wisdom in sending down this trial on him. Job pleads with Him, asking remission since life is too short; as he looks towards death, he confesses that if man's spirit departs he cannot return to life, yet he awaits his regeneration. Then, he announces that sin exposes the sinner to destruction: "My transgression is sealed up in a bag... as a mountain falls and crumbles away... So You destroy the hope of man. You prevail forever against him, and he passes on; You change his countenance and send him away" (vv. 14:17–20).

PSALMS AND GOSPELS

Matins Psalm — Psalm 27:4

This psalm speaks of longing to dwell in the house of the Lord and hear the word of salvation, as the birds of heaven nest under the mustard tree (mentioned in the Gospel message, symbolic of the kingdom of heaven): "One thing I have desired of the Lord, that will I seek: that I may dwell in the house of the Lord all the days of my life."

Matins Gospel — Luke 13:18–22

This passage speaks of the Gospel's protection for the souls of believers, where the Gospel provides immunity and growth as symbolized by the mustard seed that matured "and became a large tree, and the birds of the air nested in its branches" (v. 19).

Liturgy Psalm — Psalms 27:7–8

Speaking for penitents, who are exposed to the dangers of sinning (as the Lord of Glory was exposed to Satan's temptations in the accompanying gospel passage), this psalm pleads with God, begging His mercy and rescue: "Hear, O Lord, when I cry with my voice! Have mercy also upon me, and answer me. My heart said to You."

Liturgy Gospel Luke 4:1–13

This passage speaks of the Savior's mercy to penitents who are tried and tempted by Satan, just as He overcame him, as shown by the evangelist's saying: "Now when the devil had ended every temptation, he departed from Him until an opportune time" (v. 13).

EPISTLES

The Pauline Epistle 2 Thessalonians 2:9–17

Believers' steadfastness during temptations: In this epistle, Paul alerts believers of the tempestuous days to precede the coming of the antichrist who will precede Christ's Second Coming; thanks God who chose them from the beginning for salvation; and encourages them to remain steadfast through this temptation: "Therefore, brethren, stand fast and hold the traditions which you were taught, whether by word or our epistle" (v. 15).

The Catholic Epistle 2 Peter 2:9–15

Avoiding the wicked: At the start of this epistle, Peter announces: "The Lord knows how to deliver the godly out of temptations and to reserve the unjust under punishment for the day of judgment." Therefore, he commands believers to avoid the wicked, describing their evils as: "Having eyes full of adultery and that cannot cease from sin, enticing unstable souls" (vv. 9, 14).

The Acts Acts 28:7–11

People honoring them: In this passage, Paul and his companions received honor from Publius, the leading citizen of the Island of Malta, after Paul healed many of the sick: "They also honored us in many ways; and when we departed, they provided such things as were necessary" (v. 10).

THIRD WEEK – THURSDAY
JUDGMENT OF REPENTANCE
(Its reward on Judgment Day)

Linking the Readings:

All the readings of this day center on one theme: **Judgment of repentance** and its rewards on Judgment Day

The first prophecy speaks of **rescuing the upright from the penalty of sin**, as Lot was rescued from the destruction of Sodom and Gomorrah; the second prophecy speaks of **prolonging their lives**, as the book of Proverbs explained; and the third prophecy speaks of **comforting them**, as Isaiah promised at the coming of Christ's kingdom.

The Matins Gospel speaks of **the Savior's even-handedness in passing judgment on the penitents**, as He was even-handed in judging regarding the question on taxes; and the Liturgy Gospel speaks of **His justice in judging between the believers and unbelievers on Judgment Day**.

In the Pauline Epistle, Paul points to **justifying the penitents through faith**; in the Catholic Epistle, James reveals **the reward for their humility**; and the Acts speaks of **rescuing them from dangers**, as Paul was rescued from the viper that fastened onto his hand.

PROPHECIES

First Prophecy — Genesis 18:17–19:29[14]

Rescuing the upright from the penalty of sin: In this passage, God declared to Abraham His intention to burn Sodom and Gomorrah,

[14] This prophecy was removed in the new edition of the Katameros.

and Abraham interceded for them. Then, the two angels came to Lot, struck the people of Sodom with blindness, and took Lot out to Zoar. They destroyed Sodom and Gomorrah, and Lot's wife was turned into a pillar of salt. Summing up Lot's rescue, Scripture says: "And it came to pass, when God destroyed the cities of the plain, that God remembered Abraham, and sent Lot out of the midst of the overthrow, when He overthrew the cities in which Lot had dwelt" (v. 19:29).

Second Prophecy Proverbs 2:16–3:4

Prolonging their lives: This passage prompts the upright to cling to wisdom (meaning the law of the Gospel), keep to righteousness, avoid evil company, and walk on the straight path. Thus, revealing that clinging to wisdom fosters longevity of life: "My son, do not forget my law... for length of days and long life and peace they will add to you" (vv. 3:1–2).

Third Prophecy Isaiah 11:10–12:2

Comforting them: The start of this prophecy points to Christ's kingdom, which comes from the root of Jesse, and says, "And in that day there shall be a Root of Jesse, Who shall stand as a banner to the people; for the Gentiles shall seek Him, and His resting place shall be glorious." Then Isaiah mentions the return of the children of Israel from captivity and the call to the Gentiles, and comforts these peoples regarding their salvation [at the coming of Christ's kingdom]: "O Lord, I will praise You; though You were angry with me, Your anger is turned away, and You comfort me. Behold, God is my salvation, I will trust and not be afraid" (vv. 11:10; 12:1–2).

PSALMS AND GOSPELS

Matins Psalm — Psalms 9:11–12

The psalm begins by pointing to the response of our Lord Christ that baffled the priests' and scribes' spies, and silenced them concerning the taxes to Caesar (as mentioned in the accompanying gospel passage). Then it points to their craftiness (which He perceived) in trying to test Him with their question: "Sing praises to the Lord, who dwells in Zion! Declare His deeds among the people. When He avenges blood, He remembers them."

Matins Gospel — Luke 20:20–26

In this passage, the Savior exhibits His even-handedness in judgment, as He answered the spies of the priests and scribes regarding the question of paying taxes: "Render therefore to Caesar the things that are Caesar's, and to God the things that are God's" (v. 25).

Liturgy Psalm — Psalms 9:7–8

Alluding to the accompanying gospel passage, this psalm declares that God is just in judgment on Judgment Day to His believers and the non-believers: "But the Lord shall endure forever; He has prepared His throne for judgment. He shall judge the world in righteousness."

Liturgy Gospel — John 12:44–50

This passage speaks of the judgment of the just Savior on those who believe in Him, and on those who do not believe: "I have come as a light into the world, that whoever believes in Me should not abide in darkness... He who rejects Me, and does not receive My words, has that which judges him—the word that I have spoken will judge him in the last day" (vv. 46–48).

EPISTLES

The Pauline Epistle — Romans 4:6–11

Justifying the penitents through faith: In this epistle, Paul gives the example of Abraham in blessing those who are justified through faith, then asks if righteousness was accounted to Abraham while he was circumcised or uncircumcised, and answers that it was while he was uncircumcised, concluding that: "He received the sign of circumcision, a seal of the righteousness of the faith which he had while still uncircumcised, that he might be the father of all those who believe, though they are uncircumcised, that righteousness might be imputed to them also" (v. 11).

The Catholic Epistle — James 4:1–10

Rewarding their humility: Here, James charges believers to fight against the lust of the flesh, adultery, and pride. And in encouraging them to observe the virtue of humility, he reveals that: "God resists the proud, but gives grace to the humble" (v. 6).

The Acts — Acts 28:1–6

Rescuing them from dangers: In this passage, Paul and those with him were saved on the beach of the Island of Malta and the natives welcomed them. [On the island,] Paul was gathering wood to place on the fire, which drew out a viper (because of the heat) that fastened onto Paul's hand, yet he "shook off the creature into the fire and suffered no harm" (v. 5).

THIRD WEEK – FRIDAY
SECURITY OF REPENTANCE
(Penitents living secure from satanic assaults)

Linking the Readings:

All the readings of this day center on one theme: **Security of repentance**—penitents living a life secure from satanic assaults

The first prophecy speaks of **God's faithfulness to penitents**, as He allowed the children of Israel into the promised land for the sake of their fathers; the second prophecy speaks of **Him giving them victory over their enemies**, as He gave David victory over Saul; the third prophecy speaks of **warning them of pride**, as Isaiah warned Israel; the fourth prophecy speaks of **fleeing evil**, as Eliphaz revealed to Job; and the fifth prophecy speaks of **His commandments to the penitents**, as Jesus the son of Sirach commanded.

The Matins Gospel speaks of **raising up the penitents on judgment day**, as was revealed in the case of the woman who had seven husbands; and the Liturgy Gospel speaks of **safeguarding them**, as He safeguarded the mute man out of whom He exorcised the demon.

In the Pauline Epistle, Paul points to **the penitents' trust**, as Abraham obeyed God and went out not knowing where he was going; in the Catholic Epistle, Jude speaks of the necessity of **standing firm in the faith**; and the Acts reading speaks of **God strengthening them in hardships**, as He stood with Paul by night and strengthened him.

PROPHECIES

First Prophecy — Deuteronomy 9:7–10:11

God's faithfulness to penitents: In this prophecy, as the children of Israel are at the borders of the promised land, Moses tries to warn them against thinking that it is due to their own righteousness that they possess that land, being, as he called them, a "stiff-necked" people. Therefore, he recounts to them the events in which they provoked God's wrath by their actions: at Horeb, God would have exterminated them; when Moses ascended the mountain to receive the tablets of the covenant, they made for themselves a golden calf to worship, and His anger against Aaron would have destroyed him; at Kibroth Hattaavah, they provoked the Lord; and when He brought them to inherit the land which He gave them, they disobeyed—not having faith in Him and not listening to His voice. Despite this, Moses interceded for them before the Lord who forgave them and renewed the tablets of the covenant for them. He also separated the tribe of Levi for the lineage of the priesthood. Allowing the children of Israel into the promised land for the sake of their fathers, the Lord said to Moses: "Arise, begin your journey before the people, that they may go in and possess the land which I swore to their fathers to give them" (v. 10:11).

Second Prophecy — 1 Samuel 23:26–24:22

Giving them victory over their enemies: This passage shows that Saul and his men pursued David, who would not have escaped if not for the Philistine threat to Saul. Thereafter, after dealing with the Philistines, they returned to pursue David (who was hiding in a cave), and Saul entered this cave to attend to his needs, yet David did not wish to do him harm, but sufficed to secretly cut off the corner of his robe, and told him: "The Lord delivered you today into my hand in the cave… but my eye spared you… let the Lord avenge me on you." Saul confessed his mistake and made David swear not to cut off his descendants after him (vv. 24:10–12).

Third Prophecy Isaiah 13:2–13

Warning them of pride: This prophecy warns against pride, mentioning how the Lord gathers His army of indignation to pour out His fierce anger with full force on the whole earth: "I will punish the world for its evil, and the wicked for their iniquity; I will halt the arrogance of the proud, and will lay low the haughtiness of the terrible" (v. 11).

Fourth Prophecy Job 15:1–35

Fleeing evil: This prophecy urges the upright to avoid evil, as Eliphaz the Temanite answers Job, rebuking him for justifying himself. Then, he shows Job (based on the words of the former sages) how the life of the evildoers is turbulent: "The wicked man writhes with pain all his days… He will not be rich, nor will his wealth continue… It [his death] will be accomplished before his time, and his branch will not be green… They conceive trouble and bring forth futility; their womb prepares deceit" (vv. 20, 29, 32, 35).

Fifth Prophecy Sirach 2:1–3:4

His commandments to the penitents: This prophecy, taken from Jesus the son of Sirach (one of the Deuterocanonical books[15]), has a number of commandments directed towards the penitents, exhorting them to be patient through temptations: "Because gold is tested in fire

[15] These books, mistakenly labeled *Deuterocanonical,* have been part of the Canon since its inception; a more accurate label would be "the books removed by the Protestants when publishing the Holy Bible."

and acceptable men in the furnace of abasement"; urging them to await God's mercy: "Consider the ancient generations and see: who believed in the Lord and was put to shame[16]"; and then charging them to honor their fathers: "He that loveth God, shall obtain pardon for his sins by prayer, and shall refrain himself from them, and shall be heard in the prayer of days[17]" (vv. 2:5, 10; 3:4).

PSALMS AND GOSPELS

Matins Psalm — Psalms 16:10–11

This psalm alludes to the accompanying gospel passage in which the Savior speaks of those counted worthy to attain that age and resurrection from the dead, that they cannot "die anymore, for they are equal to the angels," and that He is not God of the dead but God of the living: "For You will not leave my soul in Sheol, nor will You allow Your Holy One to see corruption. You will show me the path of life."

Matins Gospel — Luke 20:27–38

This passage speaks of the Savior raising the righteous on judgment day, as He told the Sadducees when they asked about the woman with seven husbands: "Nor can they die anymore... being sons of the resurrection" (v. 36).

---

[16] The previous two quotes are cited from the Saint Athanasius Academy Septuagint (SAAS–2008), as found in the Orthodox Study Bible.

[17] Here the Douay-Rheims American Edition (DRA–1899) is the closest to the Coptic text; the first phrase differs, however, and the Orthodox Study Bible better matches the Coptic: "He who honors his father," which flows better with the context of the readings.

Liturgy Psalm — Psalms 16:1–2

Speaking for the man out of whom the Savior exorcised the demon, this psalm pleads with God to preserve him from the return of the demon who would bring with him seven other demons even more wicked (as mentioned in the accompanying gospel passage): "Preserve me, O God, for in You I put my trust. O my soul, you have said to the Lord, You are my Lord, my goodness is nothing apart from You."

Liturgy Gospel — Luke 11:14–26

This passage speaks of the Savior's protection of the penitents, as He safeguarded the man out of whom He exorcised the demon: "When a strong man, fully armed, guards his own palace, his goods are in peace" (v. 21).

EPISTLES

The Pauline Epistle — Hebrews 11:1–8

The penitents' trust: In this epistle, Paul defines faith as "the substance of things hoped for, the evidence of things not seen." Then, he enlists the story of Abraham as a great example of confident faith: "By faith Abraham obeyed when he was called to go out to the place which he would receive as an inheritance. And he went out, not knowing where he was going" (vv. 1, 8).

The Catholic Epistle — Jude 1:17–25

Standing firm in the faith: Here, Jude prophesies of what is to come in the end times: mockers will come walking according to their own ungodly lusts; then, he exhorts the believers to remain firm in their faith: "But you, beloved, building yourselves up on your most holy faith... keep yourselves in the love of God" (vv. 20–21).

The Acts | Acts 23:6–11

God strengthens them in hardships: This passage mentions the dispute that arose between the Sadducees and the Pharisees in the assembly because of Paul's address; and the compassion that the commander had on him lest they tear him to pieces; and finally that the Lord stood by him the following night, strengthening him, saying: "Be of good cheer, Paul; for as you have testified for Me in Jerusalem, so you must also bear witness at Rome" (v. 11).

THIRD WEEK – SATURDAY
PENITENTS' FORGIVENESS

Linking the Readings:

All the readings of this day center on one theme: **Penitents' forgiveness**—the repentant person must forgive others for his penitence to be accepted, obeying the command of the Savior: "forgive, and you will be forgiven."

The Matins Gospel speaks of **His commandment for penitents to be charitable** because it purges the soul; as He elsewhere said, "But rather give alms of such things as you have; then indeed all things are clean to you"; while the Liturgy Gospel **urges them to forgive**.

In the Pauline Epistle, Paul exhorts believers that **their sorrow should lead to repentance leading to salvation**, not as the sorrow of the world which produces death; in the Catholic Epistle, James charges them to have **faith working together with works** so as to be justified; and the Acts reading speaks of **rescuing them from dangers**, as Paul was rescued from the murder attempt plotted against him.

PSALMS AND GOSPELS

Matins Psalm — Psalms 130:1–2

Speaking for penitent believers, who do not rely on possessions (unlike the rich young man mentioned in the accompanying gospel passage) but give it in charity, the psalm pleads with God to answer their prayers and purify their souls from sin: "Out of the depths I have cried to You, O Lord; Lord, hear my voice! Let Your ears be attentive to the voice of my supplications."

Matins Gospel Mark 10:17–27

In this passage, the Savior commands believers to be charitable, so that their souls are purified, and they will have a treasure in heaven. This is shown when He said to the rich young man: "Go your way, sell whatever you have and give to the poor, and you will have treasure in heaven; and come, take up the cross, and follow Me," considering that charity purifies the soul and leads to the kingdom (v. 21).

Liturgy Psalm Psalms 27:6–8

Speaking for penitents who forgave those who wronged them (as commanded in the accompanying gospel passage), this psalm asks God to have mercy on them as they had mercy on others: "I will sing praises to the Lord. Hear, O Lord, when I cry with my voice! Have mercy also upon me, and answer me. My heart said to You."

Liturgy Gospel Matthew 18:23–35

In this passage, the Savior urges believers to forgive others, showing what the master did to the servant who would not forgive his fellow servant: he handed him over to the torturers until he pays all his debt. Then the Savior says, "So My heavenly Father also will do to you if each of you, from his heart, does not forgive his brother his trespasses" (v. 35).

EPISTLES

The Pauline Epistle 2 Corinthians 7:2–11

Believers' sorrow should lead to repentance: In this epistle, Paul expresses the consolation he felt in his tribulations when Titus returned from the Corinthians bearing the news of their sorrow—sorrow which carried them to repentance—based on Paul's previous epistle to them. Then he charges believers to imitate the Corinthians in this respect: "For godly sorrow produces repentance leading to salvation, not to be regretted; but the sorrow of the world produces death" (v. 10).

The Catholic Epistle James 2:14–26

Faith working together with works: Here, the apostle indicates that it is not befitting of believers to boast of faith that is not combined with works, showing that such faith is dead—being the faith of the demons, and not the faith of Abraham and Rahab. Then, James says candidly, "You see then that a man is justified by works, and not by faith only" (v. 24).

The Acts Acts 23:12–35

Rescue from dangers: This passage tells of the criminal conspiracy between more than forty Jews to not eat or drink until they had killed Paul, and how the commander rescued him from their hands and sent him to Felix the governor.

THIRD WEEK – SUNDAY
ACCEPTING REPENTANCE[18]

Linking the Readings:

All the readings of this day center on one theme: **Accepting repentance**

In the Vespers Gospel, the Savior **warns believers that what comes out of the mouth defiles the whole person**; in the Matins Gospel, He explains to them that **those who are chosen are few**; in the Liturgy Gospel, He **reveals that He will accept the repentance of the penitent**; and in the Evening Gospel, He declares to them that **He will raise their souls out of Hades**.

The Pauline Epistle speaks of believers' need to **be open, ready to accept penitents and forgive them**; in the Catholic Epistle, James explains to them the necessity of **taming their tongues while guiding penitents**; and the Acts reading speaks of them **not inciting the crowd in their teachings**, as Paul declared in his self-defense before the governor.

PSALMS AND GOSPELS

Vespers Psalm Psalms 88:1–2

Speaking for penitents who lift up prayers to God from their hearts (not only their lips as mentioned in the accompanying gospel passage), this psalm cries out to God to hear their prayers: "O Lord, God of my salvation, I have cried out day and night before You. Let my prayer come before You; incline Your ear to my cry."

[18] This Sunday is known as Clever-Son Sunday.

Vespers Gospel Matthew 15:1–20

In this passage, the Savior warns penitents of words that defile a man: "Not what goes into the mouth defiles a man; but what comes out of the mouth, this defiles a man" (v. 11).

Matins Psalm Psalms 55:1–2, 16

Speaking for the men of the eleventh hour who were not hired by anyone (as mentioned in the accompanying gospel passage), the start of this psalm asks God to give ear to their prayers. Then the psalm points to His response to them, and His equating them with those of the first hour (saving them): "Give ear to my prayer, O God, and do not hide Yourself from my supplication. Attend to me, and hear me; as for me, I will call upon God, and the Lord shall save me."

Matins Gospel Matthew 20:1–16

This passage shows that the Savior chooses few out of all who are invited: "For many are called, but few chosen" (v. 16).

Liturgy Psalm Psalms 79:8–9

Speaking for the lost son (mentioned in the accompanying gospel passage) who signifies the sinner who has been brought very low by the multitude of his sins, the psalm begs God to forgive his iniquities and grant him mercy: "Oh, do not remember former iniquities against us! Let Your tender mercies come speedily to meet us, for we have been brought very low. Help us, O God of our salvation, for the glory of Your name."

Liturgy Gospel Luke 15:11–32

This passage shows that the Savior accepts penitents, as illustrated by the father of the lost son who saw his son returning to him: "When he was still a great way off, his father saw him and had compassion, and ran and fell on his neck and kissed him" (v. 20).

Evening Psalm Psalms 30:1–3

This psalm points to the tax collectors and harlots who repent and precede the Jews into the kingdom (as mentioned in the accompanying gospel passage), and speaking for them, it glorifies God for accepting them: "I will extol You, O Lord, for You have lifted me up, and have not let my foes rejoice over me. O Lord my God, I cried out to You, and You healed me. O Lord, You brought my soul up from the grave."

Evening Gospel Matthew 21:28–32

This passage shows that the Savior raises penitents out of Hades, as He told the Jews who refused His call and would not believe in Him: "Assuredly, I say to you that tax collectors and harlots enter the kingdom of God before you" (v. 31).

EPISTLES

The Pauline Epistle 2 Corinthians 6:2–13

Being open: At the start of this epistle, Paul encourages the faithful to accept the grace of the Gospel with a true repentance, taking the example of the Divine Words on the tongue of Isaiah: "In an acceptable time I have heard you, and in the day of salvation I have helped you,"[19] and then Paul comments: "Behold, now is the accepted time; behold, now is the day of salvation." He proceeds to show that he is a faithful servant of Christ through the commandments he presents to them, the caution he takes in walking without offense, and what pains he endures for the Gospel. Further, he charges them: "O Corinthians! We have spoken openly to you, our heart is wide open... Now in return for the same (I speak as to children), you also be open" (vv. 2, 11–13).

The Catholic Epistle James 3:1–12

Taming the tongue while guiding penitents: Here, James charges believers to avoid exaggeration and haughtiness in correcting the brethren. He cautions to tame the tongue in speaking with them, because "no man can tame the tongue. It is an unruly evil, full of deadly poison. With it we bless our God and Father, and with it we curse men... My brethren, these things ought not to be so" (v. 8–10).

The Acts Acts 24:1–23

Not inciting the crowd in their teachings: This passage mentions the accusations brought by Tertullus, Annas the high priest, and some of the elders against Paul before the governor, and shows Paul's remarkable self-defense, in which he says: "They neither found me in the temple disputing with anyone nor inciting the crowd... unless it is for this one statement which I cried out, standing among them, 'Concerning the resurrection of the dead I am being judged by you this day.'" At this, the governor commanded to give Paul liberty and not prohibit his friends from him (vv. 12, 21).

[19] [Isaiah 49:8.]

WEEK 3: PURITY OF THE STRUGGLE (REPENTANCE)

			PSALMS & GOSPELS		*EPISTLES*		
DAY	***PROPHECIES***		**Matins**	**Liturgy**	***Pauline***	***Catholicon***	***Acts***
MONDAY: PENITENT CONFESSION	*1 **Pro**: He urges believers to confess*	*2 **Is**: The Savior reigns over them*	The Savior floods them with grace	He promises them remission of their sins	*Urging the brethren to be reconciled*	*Directing them to salvation*	*Exposure to persecutions*
TUESDAY: RIGHTEOUSNESS OF REPENTANCE	*1 **Pro**: Enlighten ment of the penitents*	*2 **Is**: He warns them against pride*	The need to reconcile disputes	He frees those who abide in His words	*Justifying penitents through faith and works*	*Loving the brethren*	*Exposure to dangers*
	*3 **Josh**: Shunning treachery*						
WEDNESDAY: TRIALS OF REPENTANCE	*1 **Ex**: God's promise to rescue the tempted*	*2 **Joel**: He consoles them*	The Gospel's protection	Experience the Savior's mercy	*Steadfast during temptations*	*Avoiding the wicked*	*People honoring them*
	*3 **Is**: Warning them against injustice*			*4 **Job**: Their future hope in Him*			
THURSDAY: JUDGEMENT OF REPENTANCE	*1 **Gen**: Rescuing the upright from sin's penalty*	*2 **Prov**: He prolongs their lives*	The Savior's even–handed judgment	The Savior's just judgment	*Justifying the penitents through faith*	*Rewarding their humility*	*Rescuing them from dangers*
	*3 **Is**: Comforting them*						
FRIDAY: SECURITY OF REPENTANCE	*1 **Deut**: God is faithful to penitents*	*2 **1 Samuel**: He conquers their enemies*	The Savior raises the righteous	The Savior protects penitents	*The penitents' trust*	*Standing firm in the faith*	*Strengthening them in hardships*
	*3 **Is**: Warning them of pride*		*4 **Job**: Fleeing evil*	*5 **Sirach**: His commandments to the penitents*			
SATURDAY: PENITENCE FORGIVENESS			He commands believers to be charitable	The Savior urges believers to forgive others	*Their sorrow should lead to repentance*	*Faith working together with works*	*Rescue from dangers*
SUNDAY: ACCEPTING REPENTANCE	**Vespers Gospel** He warns the penitents of what defiles	**Matins Gospel** The Savior chooses few	**Liturgy Gospel** The Savior accepts penitents	**Evening Gospel** The Savior raises penitents from Hades	*Being open*	*Taming the tongue while guiding penitents*	*Not inciting the crowd in their teachings*

UNIVERSAL THEME:

CREDO OF THE STRUGGLE (THE HOLY BIBLE)

FOURTH WEEK – MONDAY
SPIRIT OF THE GOSPEL
(By which believers should walk)

Linking the Readings:

All the readings of this day center on one theme: **The spirit of the Gospel**, according to which believers should walk

The first prophecy speaks of **God's blessings to those who walk according to the spirit**, as Isaac blessed Jacob rather than Esau; the second prophecy speaks of **His protection for them**, as He founded Zion to protect His faithful nation; and the third prophecy speaks of **their hope in Him**, as Job set his hope not on this [worldly] life but on death.

The Matins Gospel speaks of **the Savior's commandment to be humble**, inviting the poor to their feasts and not the rich; while in the Liturgy Gospel, **He urges them to be charitable to the poor** through whom they will be accepted into the everlasting homes.

The Pauline Epistle speaks of the believers **redeeming the body**, because they have and will have the first-fruits of the Spirit, groaning and awaiting the adoption, the redemption of their bodies; in the Catholic Epistle, James charges them to **save the souls of sinners from death** by turning them from their error; and the Acts reading encourages them to **preach the Gospel to the Gentiles** (sinners), as Peter proved in his address to those of the circumcision who contended with him.

PROPHECIES

First Prophecy — Genesis 27:1–41

God's blessings to those who walk according to the spirit: This prophecy mentions the story of Isaac sending his son Esau to hunt for him game so as to bless Esau before dying, but Rebekah toiled until Jacob [who later walked according to the spirit] received this blessing instead of his brother, which caused Esau to hate Jacob.

Second Prophecy — Isaiah 14:24–32

His protection for them: In this prophecy, God shows His intended punishment on Assyria, and His promised repayment to the Philistines for their evil. Then He mentions "that the Lord has founded Zion, and the poor of His people shall take refuge in it," showing that He had founded Zion to protect His faithful nation (v. 32).

Third Prophecy — Job 16–17

Their hope in Him: In this passage, Job rebukes his friends for their harshness; describes his misery and clings to his purity; presents them with his petition to God; shows that people's harshness on the tested startles the upright yet it does not move him; and finally declares that his hope does not hang on life, but in death: "Where then is my hope? As for my hope, who can see it? Will they go down to the gates of Sheol? Shall we have rest together in the dust?" (vv. 17:15–16).

PSALMS AND GOSPELS

Matins Psalm — Psalms 55:1; 27:7–8

Speaking for the person practicing humility and inviting the poor to his feast (as the Lord of Glory commanded in the accompanying gospel passage), this psalm asks God to answer him: "Give ear to my prayer, O God, and do not hide Yourself from my supplication. Hear, O Lord, and answer me. My heart said to You."

Matins Gospel — Luke 14:7–15

In this passage, the Savior commands believers who prepare a feast not to invite their relatives or the rich, but the poor, to be rewarded at the resurrection of the just: "When you give a feast, invite the poor, the maimed, the lame, the blind" (v. 13).

Liturgy Psalm — Psalms 55:16–17

Speaking for believers walking in the spirit of the Gospel (making friends for themselves from unrighteous mammon as mentioned in the accompanying gospel passage), this psalm confesses God's answer to their voices: "As for me, I will call upon God, and the Lord shall save me. I will pray, and cry aloud, and He shall hear my voice."

Liturgy Gospel — Luke 16:1–9

In this passage, the Savior urges believers to walk by the spirit of the Gospel, to be charitable to the poor so they would gain their reward in eternal life and enter the kingdom: "Make friends for yourselves by unrighteous mammon, that when you fail, they may receive you into an everlasting home" (v.9).

EPISTLES

The Pauline Epistle — Romans 8:12–26

Redeeming the body: In this epistle, Paul charges believers to live, not according to the flesh, but according to the spirit—comparing and contrasting both cases: "We also who have the firstfruits of the Spirit... groan within ourselves, eagerly waiting for the adoption, the redemption of our body" (v. 23).

The Catholic Epistle — James 5:16–20

Saving the souls of sinners from death: Here, James charges believers to restore those who are lost to the truth: "Brethren, if anyone among you wanders from the truth, and someone turns him back, let him know that he who turns a sinner from the error of his way will save a soul from death and cover a multitude of sins" (vv. 19–20).

The Acts — Acts 11:2–18

Preaching the Gospel to Gentiles (sinners): This passage mentions that those of the circumcision contended with Peter because he preached the Gospel to the Gentiles, to which he explained: "If therefore God gave them the same gift as He gave us when we believed on the Lord Jesus Christ, who was I that I could withstand God? When they heard these things they became silent" (vv. 17–18).

FOURTH WEEK – TUESDAY
PREACHING THE GOSPEL
(To edify the church of Christ)

Linking the Readings:

All the readings of this day center on one theme: **Preaching the Gospel** to edify the church of Christ

The first prophecy speaks of **founding the first church at the call of the Lord**, as Jacob took the stone under his head, set it up as a pillar, poured oil on it, and made it the House of God. This was after seeing the ladder in his dream and the Lord's voice calling out to him. The second prophecy speaks of **safeguarding the church**, as Isaiah spoke in his prophecy that "on this mountain the hand of the Lord will rest... He will spread out His hands in their midst" to fortify the city of Judah. The third prophecy speaks of the **darkness in the temples of the church's enemies**, as Bildad the Shuhite clarified by saying: "The light is dark in his tent, and his lamp beside him is put out." The fourth prophecy speaks of the **edification of church assemblies**, as Jesus the son of Sirach commissions believers to "let your conversation be with men of understanding, and let all your discussion be about the law of the Most High."

The Matins Gospel speaks of the **Savior's promised inheritance to those who obey His Gospel**—the kingdom of heaven—which the tax collectors and harlots gained but not the Jews. The Liturgy Gospel mentions the **conditions of preaching the Gospel**, as the Savior clarified to those who wanted to follow Him that they must leave the world behind before coming to preach the Gospel.

The Pauline Epistle speaks of **edifying the church by preaching**, as the apostle revealed that God made some apostles and some evangelists for the work of ministry, for the edifying of the body of Christ (the church) of which He is the head; the Catholic Epistle reveals that **the**

church is the means of rescue for her children, as Noah's Ark also saved those within from the flood; and the Acts reading clarifies **God's care for preachers**, as Julius treated Paul kindly and permitted him to go to his friends to receive care.

PROPHECIES

First Prophecy — Genesis 28:10–22

Founding the first church at the call of the Lord: This passage tells of the story in which Jacob dreamt of a ladder set on earth with its top reaching to heaven, and the Lord's voice calling to him, promising to give him and his descendants the land on which he was lying, so he took the stone under his head and set it up as a pillar, making it the House of God.

Second Prophecy — Isaiah 25:1–26:8

Safeguarding the church: This prophecy shows that in His church, God is "a strength to the poor, a strength to the needy in his distress, a refuge from the storm, a shade from the heat." Alluding to the sacred sacrifice in the church, he says, "And in this mountain the Lord of hosts will make for all people a feast of choice pieces, a feast of wines." Pointing to the gates of the church being open to shelter the believers, he says, "Open the gates, that the righteous nation which keeps the truth may enter in. You will keep him in perfect peace, whose mind is stayed on You, because he trusts in You." (vv. 25:4, 6; 26:2–3).

Third Prophecy Job 18:1–21

Darkness in the temples of the church's enemies: Here, Bildad the Shuhite lists the catastrophes befalling the wicked, specifically those befalling their temples: "The light is dark in his tent, and his lamp beside him is put out... They dwell in his tent who are none of his; brimstone is scattered on his dwelling... Surely such are the dwellings of the wicked, and this is the place of him who does not know God" (vv. 6, 15, 21).

Fourth Prophecy Sirach 8:1–10:1[20]

Edification of church assemblies: This prophecy urges believers to consistently attend church spiritual assemblies: "Let righteous men be your dinner companions, and let your glorying be in the fear of the Lord. Let your conversation be with men of understanding, and let all your discussion be about the law of the Most High" (RSV Sirach 9:15–16).

PSALMS AND GOSPELS

Matins Psalm Psalm 17:1

Speaking for the first son (who initially refused to go work in the vineyard but later regretted and went, as mentioned in the accompanying gospel passage), and tax collectors and harlots (who believed, though the Jews did not), this psalm begs God from a pure heart to hear their prayers: "Hear a just cause, O Lord, attend to my cry; give ear to my prayer which is not from deceitful lips."

---

[20] This prophecy seems to have been removed.

Matins Gospel Matthew 21:28–32

In this passage, the Savior promises the inheritance to those who obey the voice of the Gospel, as the first son obeyed his father's voice. The Savior answered the Jews regarding tax collectors and harlots who believed in Him: "Assuredly, I say to you that tax collectors and harlots enter the kingdom of God before you" (v. 31).

Liturgy Psalm Psalm 17:6

Speaking for the man in the accompanying gospel passage who said, "Lord I will follow You wherever You go" (representing those who want to follow Christ), this psalm asks God to hear his prayer: "I have called upon You, for You will hear me, O God; incline Your ear to me, and hear my speech."

Liturgy Gospel Luke 9:57–62

In this passage, the Savior sets conditions for those who preach the Gospel, as He told the man who excused himself to bury his father before following Him: "Let the dead bury their own dead, but you go and preach the kingdom of God" (v. 60).

EPISTLES

The Pauline Epistle Ephesians 4:1–16

Church edification by preaching: In this epistle, Paul charges believers to struggle to preserve the unity of the spirit, having one faith, showing that God gave people different gifts for the edification of the church: "And He Himself gave some to be apostles, some prophets, some evangelists, and some pastors and teachers, for the equipping of the saints for the work of ministry, for the edifying of the body of Christ" (vv. 11–12).

The Catholic Epistle 2 Peter 2:2–8

The church saves its preachers: Here, the apostle prophesies to the believers of upcoming false teachers who will bring in destructive heresies and mislead many, whose destruction does not slumber; yet believers will be saved from this destruction as Noah and those with him were saved in the ark—symbolic of the church.

The Acts Acts 27:1–3

God's care for preachers: This passage shows God's care for preachers, as it reveals that Julius the centurion "treated Paul kindly and gave him liberty to go to his friends and receive care" (v. 3).

FOURTH WEEK -WEDNESDAY
PEACE OF THE GOSPEL
(Giving the church victory over her opponents)

Linking the Readings:

All the readings of this day center on one theme: **The peace of the Gospel**—the peace surrounding the church at the Gospel's victory over her opponents

The first prophecy speaks of **God's plagues on the enemies of the church (His people)**, as He struck Pharaoh and the Egyptians with the plagues of the blood, the frogs, and the lice; the second prophecy speaks of **Him saving His people from dangers**, as He promised, on the tongue of Joel the prophet, to save the Israelites from danger; the third prophecy speaks of **believers blessing God for all the trials that come upon them**, as Job blessed God when he heard of all that befell him; and the fourth prophecy speaks of them **atoning for their iniquities, through trials**, as God contended with Israel gently when he fell, thus his iniquities were atoned for and remitted.

The Matins Gospel speaks of **the Savior condemning those who reject the Gospel**, as those who declined the invitation were deprived of tasting the banquet prepared for them; while the Liturgy Gospel speaks of the Savior **giving believers (the church) His peace by judging against those who rise up against them**, as He rebuked the wind and waves that rose up against the boat (the church) and thus there was great calm.

In the Pauline Epistle, Paul urges them to the necessity of **removing the causes of wrath from among themselves**; in the Catholic Epistle, James encourages believers to **cut off self-seeking from themselves**; and the Acts reading reveals the need to **visit the brethren in their need**.

PROPHECIES

First Prophecy Exodus 7:14–8:18

God's plagues on the enemies of the church (His people): This prophecy recalls the first three plagues (turning the Nile water into blood, the frogs filling the land, and the lice) that God sent on Pharaoh, to push him to permit the children of Israel to leave Egypt, but Pharaoh's heart was hardened and he would not listen to God's words to him, uttered by Moses and Aaron.

Second Prophecy Joel 2:28–32

Saving His people from dangers: Here, Divine Revelation, speaking on the tongue of Joel, mentions what will occur at the coming of Christ's kingdom: God will pour out His Spirit on all flesh. Next, it reveals what will occur before the coming of the great and awesome Day of the Lord: the sun will turn into darkness, the moon into blood, and "it shall come to pass that whoever calls on the name of the Lord shall be saved. For in Mount Zion and in Jerusalem there shall be deliverance," [God promised salvation from danger to the Israelites] (v. 32).

Third Prophecy Job 1:1–22

Blessing God for all the trials that come: In this passage, four servants announced the severe trials befalling Job: the Sabeans took the oxen and donkeys and killed the servants; "The fire of God fell from heaven and burned up the sheep and the servants, and consumed them;" bands raided the camels and killed the servants; and a great wind struck the four corners of the house killing his children. Yet Job endured the shocks with amazing patience and "fell to the ground and worshiped." He blessed God for all that befell him saying, "Naked I came from my mother's womb, and naked shall I return there. The Lord gave, and the Lord has taken away; blessed be the name of the Lord" (vv. 16, 20–21).

Fourth Prophecy — Isaiah 26:21–27:9

Through trials, their iniquities are atoned for: Isaiah starts by showing that God "comes out of His place to punish the inhabitants of the earth for their iniquity." Then, He speaks of His people: "In that day sing to her, 'A vineyard of red wine! I, the Lord, keep it, I water it every moment; lest any hurt it, I keep it night and day.'" He continues: "Those who come He shall cause to take root in Jacob; Israel shall blossom and bud, and fill the face of the world with fruit." He decrees that He will not strike or kill Jacob as He did to his opponents; He will contend with him if he falls, yet gently, and He will protect him from the east wind (the Babylonians). Finally, He shows His ability to atone for Jacob's iniquities: "Therefore by this the iniquity of Jacob will be covered; and this is all the fruit of taking away his sin: when he makes all the stones of the altar like chalkstones that are beaten to dust, wooden images and incense altars shall not stand" (vv. 26:21; 27:2–3, 6, 9).

PSALMS AND GOSPELS

Matins Psalm — Psalms 18:37, 40

Alluding to the accompanying gospel passage, the start of this psalm points to those who scorned the invitation to the feast (symbolic of those who scorn the preaching of the Gospel, not accepting it) and then it shows the destruction they will endure, being deprived of the feast: "I have pursued my enemies and overtaken them; neither did I turn back again till they were destroyed. You have also given me the necks of my enemies, so that I destroyed those who hated me."

Matins Gospel Luke 14:16–24

This passage shows that the Savior destroys those who refuse the invitation to the feast of the Gospel, as the host of the feast (the Lord of Glory) said to his servants regarding those who were invited: "For I say to you that none of those men who were invited shall taste my supper" (vv. 24).

Liturgy Psalm Psalms 18:17–18

Speaking for the boat, attacked by the strong winds and waves (symbolic of the church, confronted by strong enemies and rescued by the might of the Gospel—as the wind was silenced and the sea calmed at the Savior's word in the accompanying gospel passage), the psalm acknowledges to God the uprising of the enemies, and the Lord's victory for her: "He delivered me from my strong enemy, from those who hated me, for they were too strong for me. They confronted me in the day of my calamity."

Liturgy Gospel Mark 4:35–41

In this passage, the Savior gives peace to the church when enemies rise up against her, as He rebuked the wind and waves that rose up against the boat, "and the wind ceased and there was a great calm" (v. 39).

EPISTLES

The Pauline Epistle — Ephesians 4:17–32

Removing the causes of wrath: In this epistle, Paul calls believers out from the uncleanness of the Gentiles, to "put on the new man which was created according to God, in true righteousness and holiness." Next, he charges them to put off lying, and remove from themselves "all bitterness, wrath, anger, clamor, and evil speaking" (vv. 24, 31).

The Catholic Epistle — James 3:13–4:4

Cutting off self-seeking: Here, James warns them against envy and self-seeking: "For where envy and self-seeking exist, confusion and every evil thing are there," and then, he charges them to cut off the wars in their members, showing that "friendship with the world is enmity with God" (vv. 3:16; 4:4).

The Acts — Acts 11:26–12:2

Visiting the brethren in their need: The Acts reveals the believers' obligation to visit the brethren in their need, imitating the disciples' action during the extreme famine, as "each according to his ability, determined to send relief to the brethren dwelling in Judea" (v. 29).

FOURTH WEEK – THURSDAY
GOSPEL ENLIGHTENMENT

Linking the Readings:

All the readings of this day center on one theme: **Gospel enlightenment**

The first prophecy speaks of **the righteous seeing God**, as Jacob saw Him face to face in Peniel; the second prophecy speaks of **His promise to establish them**, as He promised on the mouth of Isaiah to lay a precious cornerstone in Zion so that whoever believes in Him will not be moved; the third prophecy speaks of **His woes to the wicked**, as Zophar the Naamathite admits that the joy of the wicked soon desists and an unfanned fire consumes the evil one; and the fourth prophecy speaks of **God being glorified in the righteous**, as He was glorified in Daniel when King Darius issued a decree to all his peoples to tremble and fear before the God of Daniel who preserved him from the lions.

The Matins Gospel speaks of the **demons confessing the Savior as the Son of God**; while the Liturgy Gospel speaks of **the Gospel's enlightenment to the souls of the believers**, as the Savior enlightened the vision of Bartimaeus, the blind man who had been begging.

In the Pauline Epistle, Paul speaks of the effects of the Gospel's enlightenment on **true believers' real knowledge**, as he spoke of himself: "Now I know in part, but then I shall know just as I also am known." In the Catholic Epistle, James instructs that it is a sin to teach what is right but not personally live it, because **knowing to do good deeds and not doing them is a sin**. The Acts reading speaks of **God answering the prayers of believers**, as He answered the disciples who prayed to Him when they were threatened by their opponents and "the place where they were assembled together was shaken; and they were all filled with the Holy Spirit."

PROPHECIES

First Prophecy — Genesis 32:1–30

The righteous see God: In this prophecy, Jacob sent envoys to his brother Esau (fearing his approach) and lifted up a prayer to God begging rescue from his hands; he sent Esau gifts and then struggled with the Man in 'Peniel'—noting its meaning: "For I have seen God face to face, and my life is preserved" (v. 30).

Second Prophecy — Isaiah 28:14–22

His promise to establish them: At the start of this prophecy, Isaiah rebukes Ephraim for taking refuge in lies and hiding under falsehood. Then he returns to reveal the true foundation for the faithful—the Lord Jesus: "Behold, I lay in Zion a stone for a foundation, a tried stone, a precious cornerstone, a sure foundation; whoever believes will not act hastily [will not be moved]." He then shows Ephraim that their covenant with death will be annulled and their agreement with Sheol will not stand (v. 16).

Third Prophecy — Job 20:1–29

His woes to the wicked: In this prophecy, Zophar the Naamathite describes the ways of the wicked person (forsaking and oppressing the poor, and seizing houses he did not build), then shows the end awaiting him: "An unfanned fire will consume him; it shall go ill with him who is left in his tent... The increase of his house will depart, and his goods will flow away in the day of His wrath. This is the portion from God for a wicked man, the heritage appointed to him by God" (vv. 26–29).

Fourth Prophecy Daniel 6:1–27

God glorified in the righteous: This prophecy shows that Daniel was set up as chief governor because of his loyalty. The other governors conspired against him, using a decree from King Darius that whoever petitions any god or man other than himself would be thrown in the lion's den. Then it shows that Daniel was thrown in the lion's den, yet was preserved by God. Meanwhile, his adversaries with their wives and children were thrown in the lion's den and their bones were crushed even before they reached the bottom. The passage ends, showing that the king passed a decree to his people: "In every dominion of my kingdom men must tremble and fear before the God of Daniel. For He is the living God, and steadfast forever; His kingdom is the one which shall not be destroyed, and His dominion shall endure to the end," thus, God is glorified in His righteous servants (vv. 26).

PSALMS AND GOSPELS

Matins Psalm Psalm 12:7

Speaking for believers (those released from demonic captivity as mentioned in the accompanying gospel passage) who are enlightened by the Gospel, this psalm begs God to keep and preserve them: "You shall keep them, O Lord, You shall preserve them from this generation forever."

Matins Gospel Mark 3:7–12

In this passage, demons confess the Savior as the Son of God, as the evangelist testified: "And the unclean spirits, whenever they saw Him, fell down before Him and cried out, saying, 'You are the Son of God'" (v. 11).

Liturgy Psalm Psalms 48:10–11

The start of the psalm shows the Lord of Glory's compassion on the blind man and His restoration of his vision (as mentioned in the accompanying gospel passage) and then encourages believers to rejoice in the Gospel: "Your right hand is full of righteousness. Let Mount Zion rejoice, let the daughters of Judah be glad, because of Your judgments."

Liturgy Gospel Luke 18:35–43

This passage shows that the Savior enlightens the souls of believers with the teachings of the Gospel as He enlightened the vision of Bartimaeus, the blind man who had been begging: "'Receive your sight; your faith has made you well.' And immediately he received his sight, and followed Him, glorifying God" (vv. 42–43).

EPISTLES

The Pauline Epistle 1 Corinthians 12:31–14:1

True believers' real knowledge: In this passage, the apostle reveals that the gifts, no matter how sublime, are nothing without love. Paul urges believers to practice love, pointing to its advantages: "Love never fails. But whether there are prophecies, they will fail; whether there are tongues, they will cease; whether there is knowledge, it will vanish away." He informs us that our knowledge is currently lacking, like the knowledge of children, "but when that which is perfect has come, then that which is in part will be done away." He depicts us before and after Gospel enlightenment as one who looks into a mirror: "For now we see in a mirror, dimly, but then face to face. Now

I know in part, but then I shall know just as I also am known" (vv. 13:8, 10, 12).

The Catholic Epistle James 4:11–5:3

Knowing to do good and not doing it is a sin: Here, James urges believers to abstain from speaking evil or judging one another (lest they boast of success in things pertaining to this world, forgetting that this world is passing away). Then, he charges them: "Therefore, to him who knows to do good and does not do it, to him it is sin" (v. 4:17).

The Acts Acts 4:19–31

Answering their prayers: This passage completes the previous meaning, showing that when they are threatened by what is futile, the faithful's prayers are heard. As the Jews warned Peter and John not to preach in the name of Jesus (their warnings resulting only in threats), the church resorted to praying to God for them. This prayer was answered: "The place where they were assembled together was shaken; and they were all filled with the Holy Spirit, and they spoke the word of God with boldness" (v. 31).

FOURTH WEEK – FRIDAY
FAITH IN THE GOSPEL

Linking the Readings:

All the readings of this day center on one theme: **Faith in the Gospel**

The first prophecy speaks of **the need to have faith in it**, as the Lord commanded the children of Israel to keep the commandments; the second prophecy speaks of **God's blessings to those who believe in the Holy Bible**, as He promised the poor of Israel; the third prophecy speaks of **condemning the disdainful**, as He warned the wicked on judgment day; and the fourth prophecy reveals **God glorified in those who believe in Him**, as He was glorified in Daniel when he was found safe and sound in the Lion's den.

The Matins Gospel speaks of the **power of those who believe in the Gospel to exorcise demons**, as the Savior rebuked the demon [and it came] out of the man in the synagogue; while the Liturgy Gospel speaks of **God's response to their prayers**, as the Savior answered the cries of the Canaanite woman and healed her daughter.

In the Pauline Epistle, Paul urges them to a **faithful confession of the Gospel**; in the Catholic Epistle, John commands them to the necessity of **abiding in God**; and the Acts reading urges them to **preach the Gospel to the Gentiles**.

PROPHECIES

First Prophecy — Deuteronomy 10:12–11:28

Faith in God's words by keeping the commandments: In this prophecy, Moses commissions the children of Israel to obey God's commandments (having faith in Him and His words), trying to convince them of this by reminding them of: first, the wonders that God did with them in Egypt and the wilderness; second, the blessings He promised them, such as entering the promised land and enjoying its goodness; and third, threatening them with the rain being withheld from them, and their destruction if they do not obey. Then, he commands them to study the laws and memorize them: "Behold, I set before you today a blessing and a curse: the blessing, if you obey the commandments of the Lord your God... and the curse, if you do not obey" (vv. 11:26–28).

Second Prophecy Isaiah 29:13–23

God's blessings to those who believe in the Holy Bible: At the start of this prophecy, God promises to destroy the wisdom of the wise and hide the understanding of the prudent of the children of Israel who honor Him with their lips, but distance themselves from Him with their hearts. Then, in addressing the obedient, He says: "In that day the deaf shall hear the words of the book, and the eyes of the blind shall see out of obscurity and out of darkness. The humble also shall increase their joy in the Lord, and the poor among men shall rejoice in the Holy One of Israel... Therefore thus says the Lord, who redeemed Abraham... Jacob shall not now be ashamed, nor shall his face now grow pale" (vv. 18–19, 22).

Third Prophecy Job 21:1–34

Condemning the disdainful: In this passage, Job shows how people's decisions lead them to self-harm. Sometimes the wicked prevail and so they disdain God, and sometimes their destruction is openly revealed. Furthermore, the happy and the sorrowful are equal in death. He finally decrees: "For the wicked are reserved for the day of doom; they shall be brought out on the day of wrath" (v. 30).

Fourth Prophecy Daniel 14:1[21]–42[22]

God glorified in His believers: In this prophecy, Daniel confirmed to the king that Bel [the idol] is not a true living god—not eating or drinking the provisions presented to him. Based on this, the king killed the priests who consumed the provisions, and handed Bel to Daniel to destroy. Next, Daniel refused to worship the dragon, but fed it pitch, fat, and hair until it died; consequently, the Babylonians rose up against the king, forcing him to cast Daniel into the lions' den, where Habakkuk came to him with food, and he came out safe and sound, whereas his enemies were cast into the den and destroyed. God was glorified in Daniel when the king declared, "Let all the inhabitants of the whole earth fear the God of Daniel: for he is the Savior, working signs, and wonders in the earth: who hath delivered Daniel out of the lions' den" (DRA Daniel 14:42).[23]

PSALMS AND GOSPELS

Matins Psalm Psalms 28:6–7

Speaking for the man out of whom the Savior exorcized the demon (as mentioned in the accompanying gospel passage), this psalm blesses the Lord for having mercy on him, declaring that he will place his trust in Him: "Blessed be the Lord, because He has heard the voice of my supplications! The Lord is my strength and my shield; my heart trusted in Him."

---

[21] In the Coptic text of the Holy Bible, this passage begins at verse one, while in the English translations it begins at verse two.

[22] Found in the "Deuterocanonical" Books as Bel and the Dragon.

[23] Here the Douay-Rheims American Edition (DRA–1899) is the closest to the Coptic text.

Matins Gospel Luke 4:31–37

This passage shows that the Savior exorcizes demons from believers by the power of His word: "'Be quiet, and come out of him!' And when the demon had thrown him in their midst, it came out of him and did not hurt him" (v. 35).

Liturgy Psalm Psalm 28:2

Speaking for the Canaanite woman (mentioned in the accompanying gospel passage), this psalm begs God to hear her: "Hear the voice of my supplications when I cry to You, when I lift up my hands toward Your holy sanctuary."

Liturgy Gospel Matthew 15:21–31

In this passage, the Savior responds to believers' requests, as He answered the Canaanite woman: "'O woman, great is your faith! Let it be to you as you desire.' And her daughter was healed from that very hour" (v. 28).

EPISTLES

The Pauline Epistle Hebrews 13:7–16

Faithful confession of the Gospel: In this epistle, Paul charges believers to care for the Gospel servants who guide them, warns them of strange doctrines, and commissions them to have faith in the Gospel: "Therefore by Him let us continually offer the sacrifice of praise to God, that is, the fruit of our lips, giving thanks to His name" (v. 15).

The Catholic Epistle 1 John 4:7–16

Abiding in Him: Here, John commissions believers to love one another: "If we love one another, God abides in us," proceeding further that: "God is love, and he who abides in love abides in God, and God in him" (vv. 12, 16).

The Acts Acts 22:17–24

Preaching the Gospel to the Gentiles: In his address to the Jews, Paul mentions how God called him to the apostolic service and commanded him to leave Jerusalem quickly and seek the Gentiles. The Jews caused such an uproar at the word "Gentiles," that the commander ordered him brought into the barracks (v. 21).

FOURTH WEEK – SATURDAY
KEEPING THE GOSPEL
(Faith [Friday] & Works [Saturday] go hand in hand)

Linking the Readings:

All the readings of this day center on one theme: **Keeping the Gospel**—faith (Friday) and works (Saturday) go hand in hand, applying the church doctrine that salvation is through both faith and works and not by either alone

The Matins Gospel speaks of **believers' hope in the Gospel**, as Abraham told the rich man, "They have Moses and the prophets; let them hear them," that is, their books. The Liturgy Gospel speaks of the **Savior's inheritance for them if they keep the Gospel**, as He took His kingdom from the wicked vinedressers and gave it to those who will render to him the fruits in their seasons.

In the Pauline Epistle, Paul commands believers to **live by the Gospel**, as he commanded the Philippians: "The things which you learned and received and heard and saw in me, these do." In the Catholic Epistle, James exhorts them to **be at peace with all** in obedience to the Gospel's commandments. The Acts reading speaks of **remaining steadfast in living by the Gospel** as Paul remained steadfast when confronted by the Jews.

PSALMS AND GOSPELS

Matins Psalm Psalms 142:5, 7

Speaking for poor Lazarus, who is mentioned in the accompanying gospel passage and is a symbol of believers who live by the Gospel, this psalm places all his hope in God, begging Him to save him from the prison into which the rich man was thrown: "I cried out to You, O

Lord: I said, You are my refuge, my portion in the land of the living. Bring my soul out of prison, that I may praise Your name."

Matins Gospel Luke 16:19–31

This passage speaks of hope in the Savior, to whom those who obey the Gospel cling, as Abraham told the rich man in torment concerning his brothers, to whom the rich man had asked for Lazarus to be sent, to testify of his whereabouts: "They have [the books of] Moses and the prophets; let them hear them" (v. 29).

Liturgy Psalm Psalms 61:1, 5

Speaking for believers who obey the Gospel, this psalm begs God to give them His inheritance (His kingdom), as mentioned in the accompanying gospel passage: "Hear my cry, O God; attend to my prayer. You have given me the heritage of those who fear Your name."

Liturgy Gospel Matthew 21:33–46

This passage shows that the Savior grants His inheritance to those who live by the Gospel, as He told the high priests and Pharisees about the wicked vinedressers in the parable of the vineyard: "I say to you, the kingdom of God will be taken from you and given to a nation bearing the fruits of it" (v. 43).

EPISTLES

The Pauline Epistle — Philippians 4:4–9

Living by the Gospel: In this epistle, Paul charges believers to always meditate on what is pure and noble, continuing: "The things which you learned and received and heard and saw in me, these do, and the God of peace will be with you" (v. 9).

The Catholic Epistle — James 3:13–4:6

Being at peace with all: In this epistle, James reaffirms the previous theme: "For where envy and self-seeking exist, confusion and every evil thing are there. But the wisdom that is from above is first pure, then peaceable... Now the fruit of righteousness is sown in peace by those who make peace" (vv. 3:16–18).

The Acts — Acts 24:24–25:12

Remaining steadfast in living by the Gospel: This passage shows that Paul preached Christ the Master to Felix the governor and his wife. Felix awaited a bribe from Paul to release him, but when this hope failed, he left him in prison. When Festus came into the province, the Jews accused Paul, who took to defending himself saying: "For if I am an offender, or have committed anything deserving of death, I do not object to dying; but if there is nothing... no one can deliver me to them" (v. 25:11).

FOURTH WEEK – SUNDAY
GOSPEL STRENGTH
(Gospel strength to keepers of its laws)

Linking the Readings:

All the readings of this day center on one theme: **Gospel strength**—the Gospel strengthens those who keep its precepts

The Vespers Gospel speaks of the **Savior's inheritance to those who seek His Gospel**, as He promised if they seek the kingdom of God; the Matins Gospel speaks of Him **selecting them**, as He declared: "For many are called, but few are chosen"; the Liturgy Gospel speaks of **His Gospel's strength in them**, as He promised: "Whoever drinks of the water that I shall give him will never thirst"; and the Evening Gospel speaks of **His mercy on them**, instructing them until the time comes for His laws and for worshipping Him in spirit and truth.

The Pauline Epistle exhorts them to **be armed with the word of the Gospel**, as the Apostle calls it "the sword of the Spirit, which is the word of God"; in the Catholic Epistle, James warns them of the **sin of not abiding by the Gospel**; and the Acts reading points to the **preachers' strength in self-defense**, as did Paul.

PSALMS AND GOSPELS

Vespers Psalm — Psalms 27:14, 13

This psalm urges believers to await the Lord's help with courage, patience, and steadfastness, alluding to the accompanying gospel passage in which God gives them spiritual gifts if they seek His Kingdom: "Wait on the Lord; be of good courage, and He shall strengthen your heart; wait, I say, on the Lord! I had believed that I would see the goodness of the Lord in the land of the living."

Vespers Gospel Luke 12:22–31

This passage shows that the Savior grants gifts to those who seek the Kingdom of God, as He says: "But seek the kingdom of God, and all these things shall be added to you" (v. 31).

Matins Psalm Psalms 31:24, 23

The start of this psalm urges those who rely on God to be of good courage, and then alludes to the accompanying gospel passage in which He chooses few out of those who are invited: "Be of good courage, and He shall strengthen your heart, all you who hope in the Lord. Oh, love the Lord, all you His saints! For the Lord preserves the faithful."

Matins Gospel Matthew 22:1–14

This passage speaks of the Savior choosing those who rely on Him, as He said in the parable of the king who arranged a feast for his son: "For many are called, but few are chosen" (v. 14).

Liturgy Psalm Psalms 105:3–5

This psalm encourages believers to continually seek the Lord's face, and points to the strength of those who accept and keep the Gospel, never thirsting forever: "Let the hearts of those rejoice who seek the Lord! Seek the Lord and His strength; seek His face evermore! Remember His marvelous works which He has done, His wonders, and the judgments of His mouth."

Liturgy Gospel John 4:1–42

This passage shows that the Savior gives strength to those who walk according to the Gospel, as He told the Samaritan woman: "But whoever drinks of the water that I shall give him will never thirst" (v. 14).

Evening Psalm Psalms 32:10–11

The start of this psalm alludes to the accompanying gospel passage in which the Samaritans worship what they do not know, but believers know what they worship. It shows that the first will suffer sorrows while the others will receive mercy and then charges believers to rejoice: "Many sorrows shall be to the wicked; but he who trusts in the Lord, mercy shall surround him. Be glad in the Lord and rejoice, you righteous; and shout for joy, all you upright in heart!"

Evening Gospel John 4:19–24

This passage speaks of the Savior's mercy on those who rely on Him, instructing them that the time for His law and worship has come, as He said: "But the hour is coming, and now is, when the true worshipers will worship the Father in spirit and truth; for the Father is seeking such to worship Him" (v. 23).

EPISTLES

The Pauline Epistle Ephesians 6:10–24

Being armed with the Gospel: In this epistle, Paul shows that our life on earth is a continual state of warfare (not against the flesh, but against spiritual enemies); therefore, Paul charges us to put on the armor of God to be able to withstand the wiles of the devil. Then he describes the whole armor of God, including, "the sword of the Spirit, which is the word of God" (v. 17).

The Catholic Epistle James 4:7–17

The sin of not abiding by the Gospel: Here, James charges believers to put aside pride, speaking evil of one another, or judging others—lest they boast in their worldly success and forget that this life is transitory. Then James says: "Therefore, to him who knows to do good and does not do it, to him it is sin" (v. 17).

The Acts Acts 25:13–26:1

Gospel preachers' strength in self-defense: In this passage, Festus presented the case of Paul to King Agrippa and called Paul into his presence, declaring that he has done nothing deserving of death, to which the king responded: "You are permitted to speak for yourself" (v. 26:1).

WEEK 4: CREDO OF THE STRUGGLE (THE HOLY BIBLE)

			PSALMS & GOSPELS		***EPISTLES***		
DAY	***PROPHECIES***		**Matins**	**Liturgy**	***Pauline***	***Catholicon***	***Acts***
MONDAY: SPIRIT OF THE GOSPEL	*1* ***Gen****: His blessings to those who walk in the spirit*	*2* ***Is****: His protection for them*	The Savior commands to be humble	He urges them to be charitable to the poor	*Redeeming the body*	*Saving sinners' souls from death*	*Preaching the Gospel to Gentiles*
	3 ***Job****: Their hope in Him*						
TUESDAY: PREACHING THE GOSPEL	*1* ***Gen****: Founding the first church*	*2* ***Is****: He safeguards the church*	His promised inheritance to Gospel adherers	Conditions for preaching the Gospel	*Church edification by preaching*	*The Church saves its preachers*	*God's care for preachers*
	3 ***Job****: Darkness in temples of church enemies*			*4* ***Sir****: Edification of Church assemblies*			
WEDNESDAY: PEACE OF THE GOSPEL	*1* ***Ex****: God's plagues on church enemies*	*2* ***Joel****: Saving His people from dangers*	He condemns those who reject the Gospel	The Savior gives the Church His peace	*Removing the causes of wrath*	*Cutting off self-seeking*	*Visiting the brethren in their need*
	3 ***Job****: Blessing God for all the trials that come*			*4* ***Is****: Atoning for people's iniquities through trials*			
THURSDAY: GOSPEL ENLIGHTENMENT	*1* ***Gen****: The righteous see God*	*2* ***Is****: His promise to establish them*	Demons confess the Savior as the Son of God	He enlightens believers' souls	*Believers' real knowledge*	*Knowing to do good*	*Answering their prayers*
	3 ***Job****: His woes to the wicked*			*4* ***Dan****: God is glorified in the righteous*			
FRIDAY: FAITH IN THE GOSPEL	*1* ***Deut****: Faith in God's words*	*2* ***Is****: God's blessings to Bible believers*	Power of Gospel-believers to exorcise demons	God's response to their prayers	*Faithful confession of the Gospel*	*Abiding in Him*	*Preaching the Gospel to the Gentiles*
	3 ***Job****: Condemning the disdainful*			*4* ***Dan****: God is glorified in His believers*			
SATURDAY: KEEPING THE GOSPEL			Believers' hope in the Savior	The Savior's inheritance for them	*Living by the Gospel*	*Being at peace with all*	*Steadfast in living by the Gospel*
SUNDAY: GOSPEL STRENGTH	**Vespers Gospel** Gospel seekers' inheritance	**Matins Gospel** The Savior choosing them	**Liturgy Gospel** His Gospel's strength in them	**Evening Gospel** His mercy on them	*Being armed with the Gospel*	*The sin of not abiding by the Gospel*	*Gospel preachers' strength in self-defense*

PART II: FRUITS OF THE STRUGGLE

UNIVERSAL THEME:

Goal of the Struggle (Faith)

FIFTH WEEK – MONDAY
RELIANCE ON FAITH
(Believers rely on God)

Linking the Readings:

All the readings of this day center on one theme: **Reliance on faith—** believers' reliance on God

In the first prophecy, wisdom (symbolic of faith) commands **believers to submit to her commandments** because "Length of days is in her right hand, in her left hand riches and honor"; in the second prophecy Isaiah assures them of **the relationship between righteousness and length of days** (as wisdom mentioned in the first prophecy), as the life of the righteous King Hezekiah was lengthened by fifteen years; and in the third prophecy Eliphaz the Temanite shows what **riches and honor await them** (as the first prophecy stated) as he told Job, "Yes, the Almighty will be your gold... And lift up your face to God."

In the Matins Gospel, the Savior **alerts believers that God removes those who rely on their possessions**—those who hoard for themselves and are not rich toward God—as He destroyed the man whose land yielded plentifully; while in the Liturgy Gospel, He **satiates believers who rely on Him with the nourishment of the Gospel**, as He filled the multitudes who gathered around Him with the five loaves and the two fish.

In the Pauline Epistle, Paul commands them to fulfill his **joy by keeping the unity and humility** as Christ the Master also did; in the Catholic Epistle, Peter blesses them if they **suffer for righteousness' sake**; and in the Acts reading, he reveals to them (as he revealed in his speech to

Cornelius and his companions) that "**God shows no partiality**. But in every nation whoever fears Him and works righteousness is accepted by Him."

PROPHECIES

First Prophecy — Proverbs 3:5–18

Believers' reliance on God: In this passage, the Sage commands believers not to be wise in their own eyes, but to trust in God. Then he blesses those who find wisdom (symbolic of faith) and shows her blessings: "Her proceeds are better than the profits of silver, and her gain than fine gold... Length of days is in her right hand, in her left hand riches and honor...And all her paths are peace" (vv. 14–17).

Second Prophecy — Isaiah 37:33–38:6

He gives them length of days: In this passage (which shows that in the right hand of Wisdom is length of days, as mentioned in the previous prophecy), Isaiah prophesies what is to become of Sennacherib and his army who are besieging Jerusalem (the angel kills 185,000 of the army, and Sennacherib is killed by his sons for his evil). Then the prophecy shows the prayer that the righteous king Hezekiah offered while on his deathbed, weeping bitterly, and that Isaiah returned and brought the good news of God's answer to his prayer, in which He increased his life fifteen years for Hezekiah's righteousness and loyal heart.

Third Prophecy — Job 22:1–30

His riches and honor await them: While the previous prophecy shows that wisdom's right hand prolongs days, this prophecy reveals that on wisdom's left are riches and honor (as also mentioned in the first prophecy). So here Eliphaz the Temanite shows Job that human righteousness is not profitable to God, but to one's own self. He then accuses Job of many iniquities and urges him to repent—which leads to great mercies from God, such as riches and honor, saying to him: "If you return to the Almighty, you will be built up... Yes, the Almighty will be your gold and your precious silver... You will make your prayer to Him, He will hear you... So light will shine on your ways" (vv. 23–28).

PSALMS AND GOSPELS

Matins Psalm — Psalms 88:2–4

Speaking for believers who feel the weight of their iniquities and fear the same fate as the rich fool (mentioned in the accompanying gospel passage), this psalm begins by asking God to answer their cry. Then it shows the end of that rich fool: "Incline Your ear to my cry. For my soul is full of troubles, and my life draws near to the grave. I am counted with those who go down to the pit."

Matins Gospel — Luke 12:16–21

In this passage, the Savior terminates the lives of those who rely on money, as God told the rich fool: "Fool! This night your soul will be required of you... [And the Savior remarked] So is he who lays up treasure for himself, and is not rich toward God" (vv. 20–21).

Liturgy Psalm — Psalms 86:3–4

Speaking for the multitudes who rely on the Lord Jesus and who sat listening to His teachings all day long (alluding to the Gospel passage and symbolic of believers who rely on God while in danger of perishing in the wilderness of this world), this psalm asks God to send down His Gospel blessings to them because they have lifted up their souls to Him and says: "Be merciful to me, O Lord, for I cry to You all day long. Rejoice the soul of Your servant, for to You, O Lord, I lift up my soul."

Liturgy Gospel Luke 9:12–17

This passage shows that the Savior satiates believers who rely on Him with nourishment from the Gospel, as He did with the multitudes who surrounded Him and listened to Him all day long, by blessing the five loaves and the two fish, "So they all ate and were filled, and twelve baskets of the leftover fragments were taken up by them" (v.17).

EPISTLES

The Pauline Epistle Philippians 2:1–16

Keeping the unity and humility: In this epistle, Paul charges believers to fulfill his joy by being cautious to be united and humble: "Being like-minded, having the same love, being of one accord, of one mind. Let nothing be done through selfish ambition or conceit, but in lowliness of mind let each esteem others better than himself." He then gives them the example of Christ the Master who: "Being found in appearance as a man, He humbled Himself and became obedient to the point of death, even the death of the cross," and encourages them to be blameless, "holding fast the word of life" (vv. 2–3, 8, 16).

The Catholic Epistle 1 Peter 3:10–18

Suffering for righteousness' sake (the faith): Here, Peter encourages them to avoid evil and do good, blessing them if they suffer for righteousness' sake: "For it is better, if it is the will of God, to suffer for doing good than for doing evil," using Christ the Master as an example who: "Also suffered once for sins, the just for the unjust, that He might bring us to God, being put to death in the flesh but made alive by the Spirit" (vv. 17, 18).

The Acts Acts 10:25–35

Accepting Gentile believers without partiality: This passage shows Peter going to meet Cornelius (a Gentile) who told Peter: "Now therefore, we are all present before God, to hear all the things commanded you by God," to which Peter answered, "In truth I perceive that God shows no partiality. But in every nation whoever fears Him and works righteousness is accepted by Him" (vv. 33–35).

FIFTH WEEK – TUESDAY
THE MINISTRY OF FAITH
(Believers shouldering faith-ministry)

Linking the Readings:

All the readings of this day center on one theme: Believers shouldering **faith-ministry**

The first prophecy speaks of **servants participating in faith-ministry**, as God took of the Spirit upon Moses and placed the same on the seventy elders chosen from the people, so that they prophesied. The second prophecy speaks of **faith-ministry's grace**, as was said of wisdom in Solomon's Proverbs: "She will place on your head an ornament of grace." The third prophecy speaks of **Gospel-ministry's eternal endurance**, as Isaiah testified: "The word of our God stands forever." The fourth prophecy speaks of **the world's corruptness in contrast**, as Bildad the Shuhite asked, "How then can man be righteous before God?" And the fifth prophecy speaks of **God's unfathomable power revealed in faith-ministry**, as Job asked, "But the thunder of His power who can understand?"

The Matins Gospel speaks of the **Savior's mercy on the weak in faith**, as He asked the father of the son afflicted with the mute spirit (which the disciples were unable to exorcise) to believe; while the Liturgy Gospel speaks of **Him personally serving in the temple**.

In the Pauline Epistle, Paul reveals the importance of **Gospel-ministers' faithfulness**, as Timothy and Epaphroditus served loyally and faithfully; in the Catholic Epistle, John urges them on the necessity of **loving one another**; and in the Acts reading, Paul exhorts them concerning the need to **defend the faith**, as he did before the governor.

PROPHECIES

First Prophecy — Numbers 10:35–11:34

Servants participating in faith-ministry: This passage mentions that the people of Israel complained against Moses in the wilderness because of their desire for meat, and Moses complained to God about bearing the burden of all this great nation alone, so he chose 70 elders of the people (according to God's command) to bear the burden with him: "Then the Lord came down in the cloud, and spoke to him, and took of the Spirit that was upon him, and placed the same upon the seventy elders; and it happened, when the Spirit rested upon them, that they prophesied" [fellowship alleviates the burden] (v. 11:25).

Second Prophecy — Proverbs 3:19–4:9

Faith-ministry grace: This passage speaks of the might of wisdom (symbolic of faith) and its benefits, encouraging the wise to do good, be peaceable, and be content. It reveals the evil fate of the wicked, and finally, urges believers to seek wisdom, saying to those who find it: "She will bring you honor, when you embrace her. She will place on your head an ornament of grace; a crown of glory she will deliver to you" (vv. 4:8–9).

Third Prophecy — Isaiah 40:1–8

Faith-ministry's eternal endurance: The start of this prophecy points to the spread of the Gospel and then speaks of the ministry of John the Baptist. Isaiah concludes that the word of faith endures: "The grass withers, the flower fades, but the word of our God stands forever" (v. 8).

Fourth Prophecy Job 25:1–6

The world's corruptness in contrast: In this short passage, Bildad the Shuhite declares to Job that God shines His light on all, and a human cannot be righteous in His presence: "How then can man be righteous before God? Or how can he be pure who is born of a woman?" (v. 4).

Fifth Prophecy Job 26:1–14

God's unfathomable power revealed in faith-ministry: In this passage, Job answers, rebuking Bildad the Shuhite for the ungracious spirit he attributed to God, confessing the unlimited, unfathomable capacity of the Most High: "Indeed these are the mere edges of His ways, and how small a whisper we hear of Him! But the thunder of His power who can understand?" (v. 14).

PSALMS AND GOSPELS

Matins Psalm Psalms 86:5–6

Speaking for the demon-possessed boy's father (whose story is in the accompanying gospel passage), this psalm cries out to God, supplicating Him to answer his prayer: "For You, Lord, are good, and ready to forgive, and abundant in mercy to all those who call upon You. Give ear, O Lord, to my prayer; and attend to the voice of my supplications."

Matins Gospel Mark 9:14–24

In this passage, the Savior reveals His mercy to the weak in faith, as He told the man who asked Him to exorcise the mute spirit from His son: "If you can believe, all things are possible to him who believes" (v. 23).

Liturgy Psalm Psalm 86:17

This psalm alludes to the accompanying gospel passage in which the Pharisees told the Savior: "You bear witness of Yourself; Your witness is not true," and speaks for the Savior, asking the Father to reveal to them (through a sign) not to judge according to the flesh (as He instructed them): "Show me a sign for good, that those who hate me may see it and be ashamed."

Liturgy Gospel John 8:12–20

This passage shows that the Savior ministered in the temple, as the evangelist testified: "These words Jesus spoke in the treasury, as He taught in the temple; and no one laid hands on Him, for His hour had not yet come" (v. 20).

EPISTLES

The Pauline Epistle Philippians 2:22–26

Gospel–ministers' faithfulness: In this epistle, Paul promises the Philippians that he will shortly send to them Timothy, the faithful servant, of whom he says: "As a son with his father he served with me in the gospel," also preparing them by sending "Epaphroditus, my brother, fellow worker, and fellow soldier" (vv. 22, 25).

The Catholic Epistle 1 John 3:2–11

Loving one another: After showing the greatness of God's love, through which He called us His children, John charges us to obey the Lord's commandments because, "Whoever has been born of God does not sin... Whoever does not practice righteousness is not of God, nor is he who does not love his brother. For this is the message that you heard from the beginning, that we should love one another" (vv. 9–11).

The Acts Acts 24:10–23

Defending the faith: This passage shows that Paul stood before Felix the governor defending himself and his Gospel, overturning the accusations of Ananias the high priest, the elders, and Tertullus the orator. In his defense, he said: "They ought to have been here before you to object if they had anything against me. Or else let those who are here themselves say if they found any wrongdoing in me while I stood before the council, unless it is for this one statement which I cried out, standing among them, 'Concerning the resurrection of the dead I am being judged by you this day'" (vv. 19–21).

FIFTH WEEK – WEDNESDAY
HOPE OF FAITH
(Hope of salvation that produces faith)

Linking the Readings:

All the readings of this day center on one theme: **Hope of faith**—the hope of salvation that faith produces in believers

The first prophecy urges **believers to hope in the fruit of faith**, as Moses and his people hoped that the plagues that God brought down on Pharaoh would soften his hard-heartedness, so that he would release the children of Israel; the second prophecy promises them **God's security to them**, as He promised Israel on the tongue of Isaiah, saying, "Fear not, for I am with you"; the third prophecy reveals **God's blessings for them**, as He told Israel on the tongue of Joel: "And it will come to pass in that day that the mountains shall drip with new wine, the hills shall flow with milk"; the fourth prophecy **urges them to live in wisdom (the fear of God)**, as Job termed it; the fifth prophecy commands them to **avoid the path of the wicked**, as Solomon commanded in the Proverbs; and the sixth prophecy reveals the Lord **blessing the believers' descendants**, as He visited barren Hannah and her husband Elkanah through the prayers of Eli the priest, so they had three sons and two daughters other than Samuel.

In the Matins Gospel, the Savior instructs them to **be bound to Him through the Gospel** [the bond of faith], which binds the church (the believers) with her Bridegroom (Christ), as the holy mystery of matrimony binds the groom with his bride—an unbreakable bond. In the Liturgy Gospel, He reveals to them **His patience with the unfruitful fig tree** for another year before He cuts it down; perhaps, it will be fruitful after He digs around it and fertilizes it.

In the Pauline Epistle, Paul urges them to have **confidence in the hope of faith, which does not fail, even amid hardships**; in the Catholic

Epistle, Peter offers **believers consolation amid tribulations, for thus they are being glorified with Christ the Master**; and then he reveals to them, in the Acts reading, the salvation that they will gain, as **the Gentiles gained salvation**.

PROPHECIES

First Prophecy Exodus 8:20–9:35

Believers' hope in God's might: This prophecy shows God bringing down plagues four to seven (swarms of flies, pestilence, boils, and hail) on Pharaoh, so that he would release the children of Israel, yet Pharaoh's heart returned hardened after each plague. However, Moses and his people had firm hope that God's might would work in him, which actually occurred after the tenth plague.

Second Prophecy Isaiah 41:4–14

God's security to them: At the start of this prophecy, the Lord recounts His mercy on the church and then He floods her with His promises: "'But you, Israel, are My servant, Jacob whom I have chosen... Fear not, for I am with you... Fear not, you worm Jacob, you men of Israel! I will help you,' says the Lord" (vv. 8, 10, 14).

Third Prophecy Joel 3:9–21

God's blessings to them: At the start of this prophecy, God judges the nations for their overflowing wickedness and then states, "But the Lord will be a shelter for His people, and the strength of the children of Israel," frankly pointing to His blessings to them: "And it will come to pass in that day that the mountains shall drip with new wine, the hills shall flow with milk, and all the brooks of Judah shall be flooded with water; a fountain shall flow from the house of the Lord and water the Valley of Acacias" (vv. 16, 18).

Fourth Prophecy Job 28:12–28

Urging them to live in wisdom (the fear of God): At the start of this passage, Job shows that humans have knowledge of natural matters, such as silver, gold, iron, etc., but then he thinks and asks: "But where can wisdom be found? And where is the place of understanding?" Showing wisdom's magnificence, Job says: "The topaz of Ethiopia cannot equal it, nor can it be valued in pure gold," declaring, "God understands its way, and He knows its place," frankly saying what God said to man: "Behold, the fear of the Lord, that is wisdom, and to depart from evil is understanding" (vv. 12, 19, 23, 28).

Fifth Prophecy Proverbs 4:10–19

Avoiding the path of the wicked: This prophecy completes the meaning of the previous prophecy, guiding the wise to sidestep the path of the wicked, saying clearly: "Do not enter the path of the wicked, and do not walk in the way of evil. Avoid it, do not travel on it; turn away from it and pass on" (vv. 14–15).

Sixth Prophecy 1 Samuel 1:1–2:21[24]

Blessing their descendants: This passage relates the story of Elkanah and his wives, Hannah and Peninnah, and shows how God answered the prayer of barren Hannah by giving her Samuel whom she gave to the Lord, thereby fulfilling her vow that he would serve the Lord. Finally, the prophecy shows that Eli the priest blessed Elkanah and his wife: "'The Lord give you descendants from this woman for the loan

---

[24] The prophecy seems to have been removed from the readings.

[Samuel] that was given to the Lord'... And the Lord visited Hannah, so that she conceived and bore three sons and two daughters" (vv. 2:20–21).

PSALMS AND GOSPELS

Matins Psalm Psalms 55:1–2

Speaking for the believer who is living on the hope of faith and who begs God that he may continue bound to Him, as the man is bound to his wife (mentioned in the accompanying gospel passage), the psalm asks God to answer his prayer: "Give ear to my prayer, O God, and do not hide Yourself from my supplication. Attend to me, and hear me."

Matins Gospel Mark 10:1–12

This passage speaks of the bond of faith that binds believers (the church—the body of Christ) to the Head who is the Savior Himself, as the Sacrament of Holy Matrimony binds the man and the woman—an indivisible bond, as the Savior instructed the Pharisees: "Therefore what God has joined together, let not man separate" (v. 9).

Liturgy Psalm Psalms 86:13–14

Speaking for the believer who lives on the hope of faith, this psalm confesses God's mercy because he saved him from eternal death (as the owner of the vineyard waited another year for the unfruitful fig tree in the accompanying gospel passage), and asks God to save him from the enemies of faith who rose up against him: "For great is Your mercy toward me, and You have delivered my soul from the depths of Sheol. O God, the proud have risen against me."

Liturgy Gospel Luke 13:6–9

This passage shows the Savior's patience towards believers who have not yet born fruit, who can be pruned by the holy books, as the vinedresser hoped for the fig tree to bring forth fruit after he digs around it and fertilizes it, as he told the vineyard owner: "Sir, let it alone this year also, until I dig around it and fertilize it. And if it bears fruit, well. But if not, after that you can cut it down" (vv. 8–9).

EPISTLES

The Pauline Epistle Romans 4:14–5:5

Confidence in the hope of faith: In this epistle, Paul shows that through faith Abraham and his seed received the promise and Abraham became the father of all believers. We, likewise, will be justified through faith. Based on this justification in Him, we will have peace with God through Jesus Christ: "Through whom also we have access by faith into this grace in which we stand, and rejoice in hope of the glory of God. And not only that, but we also glory in tribulations, knowing that tribulation produces perseverance; and perseverance, character; and character, hope. Now hope does not disappoint" (vv. 5:2–5).

The Catholic Epistle 1 Peter 4:12–19

Believers' consolation in Him: Here, Peter consoles believers in trials: "Rejoice to the extent that you partake of Christ's sufferings, that when His glory is revealed, you may also be glad with exceeding joy." He then blesses them for being reproached for the name of Christ, and charges each one not to suffer as a murderer, thief, or evildoer, but as a Christian: "For the time has come for judgment to begin at the house of God; and if it begins with us first, what will be the end of those who do not obey the gospel of God?" (vv. 13, 17).

The Acts Acts 11:12–18

Gentiles gain salvation: In this passage, Peter offered his defense when those of the circumcision disputed with him because he went to the Gentiles and ate with them: "The Holy Spirit descended upon them, 'If therefore God gave them the same gift as He gave us when we believed on the Lord Jesus Christ, who was I that I could withstand God?' When they heard these things they became silent; and they glorified God, saying, 'Then God has also granted to the Gentiles repentance to life'" (vv. 17–18).

FIFTH WEEK – THURSDAY
FREEDOM OF FAITH
(Saving believers' souls from Satan)

Linking the Readings:

All the readings of this day center on one theme: **Freedom of faith**—which saves believers' souls from imprisonment to Satan and slavery to sin

In the first prophecy, divine revelation speaks on the mouth of Isaiah of **the Savior's efforts to loosen the bonds of believers**; the second prophecy **urges them to holiness**, as Solomon commanded in Proverbs to keep the commandments because in them is life to the soul and health to the body; in the third prophecy **they yearn to return to their former spiritual glory**, as Job longed for his former glory; and in the fourth prophecy, **He empowers them spiritually**, as Samuel grew until "all Israel ...knew that Samuel had been established as a prophet of the Lord."

In the Matins Gospel, **the Savior exorcizes the unclean spirit from them**, as He exorcized it from the father's only child; and in the Liturgy Gospel, **He loosens the bonds of Satan from them**, as He loosed them from the hunchback woman bound by this spirit for eighteen years.

In the Pauline Epistle, Paul commands them to **flee idolatrous worship and refuse the table of demons**; in the Catholic Epistle, Peter urges them to **bless God for the grace of their salvation through Christ Jesus**; and in the Acts reading, Paul exhorts them not only to be ready to be bound, but also to be **ready to die for the sake of the name of Jesus Christ**, as he personally testified.

PROPHECIES

First Prophecy — Isaiah 42:5–16

The Savior's efforts to loosen the bonds of believers: Isaiah, the evangelical prophet, prefaces the selected prophecy with Christ the Master's humble steadfast work: "Till He has established justice in the earth; and the coastlands shall wait for His law." Then, in this passage, he begins to reveal the Lord's covenant with the believers in and through Him: "I will... give You as a covenant to the people, as a light to the Gentiles, to open blind eyes, to bring out prisoners from the prison, those who sit in darkness from the prison house." Finally, he charges them to sing a new praise for the faith that made "darkness light before them, and crooked places straight" (vv. 4, 6–7, 16).

Second Prophecy — Proverbs 4:20–27[25]

Urging them to holiness: Here, the Sage directs believers to keep the commandments of faith, "for they are life to those who find them, and health to all their flesh" (life for the souls and health to the bodies). Then he urges them to pursue holiness: "Keep your heart with all watchfulness, for from these words are the issues of life... turn your foot from an evil way; for God knows the ways on the right hand, but those on the left are perverse" (vv. 22, 23, 27).

Third Prophecy — Job 29:2–20

Yearning for their former spiritual glory: In this passage, Job regrets his lost prestige and glory, wishing its return: "Oh, that I were as in

---

[25] The following verse appears in the old and new Katameros; it can be found in the Septuagint translation as the continuation of verse 27: "For God knows the ways on the right hand, but those on the left are perverse; and He shall make your paths straight, and guide your steps in peace."

months past, as in the days when God watched over me; when His lamp shone upon my head, and when by His light I walked through darkness." Then, he remembers God's past blessings: "When my steps were bathed with cream, and the rock poured out rivers of oil for me," attributing them to his charity: "I was eyes to the blind, and I was feet to the lame. I was a father to the poor… I broke the fangs of the wicked, and plucked the victim from his teeth" (vv. 2–3, 6, 15–17).

Fourth Prophecy 1 Samuel 3:1–20[26]

Empowering them spiritually: This prophecy shows how God's word was revealed to Samuel for the first time, when He told him of the destruction to the house of Eli the priest, and how Eli received this news. Then the prophecy shows how Samuel grew, "and the Lord was with him and let none of his words fall to the ground. And all Israel from Dan to Beersheba knew that Samuel had been established as a prophet of the Lord" (vv. 19–20).

PSALMS AND GOSPELS

Matins Psalm Psalm 86:14

This psalm alludes to the accompanying gospel passage, in which the disciples were unable to exorcize the unclean spirit from the father's only child, so the Savior rebuked their lack of faith: "O God, the proud have risen against me, and a mob of violent men have sought my life, and have not set You before them."

[26] This prophecy seems to have been removed.

Matins Gospel Luke 9:37–43

This passage speaks of the Savior exorcizing the unclean spirit from believers by His power, as the Gospel said about Him: "Then Jesus rebuked the unclean spirit, healed the child, and gave him back to his father" (v. 42).

Liturgy Psalm Psalm 86:17

The psalm points to the sign Jesus did (healing the hunchback woman), and the shame the scoffers felt after they derided Him in the synagogue for performing this sign on the Sabbath (as mentioned in the accompanying gospel passage): "Show me a sign for good, that those who hate me may see it and be ashamed, [because You, Lord, have helped me and comforted me]."

Liturgy Gospel Luke 13:10–17

This passage speaks of loosening the bonds of Satan, which the Savior did by His power to help the believers, as He told the Jews who derided Him for healing the hunchback woman on the Sabbath: "So ought not this woman, being a daughter of Abraham, whom Satan has bound—think of it—for eighteen years, be loosed from this bond on the Sabbath?" (v. 16).

EPISTLES

The Pauline Epistle 1 Corinthians 10:14–11:1

Fleeing idolatrous worship and refusing the table of demons: In this epistle, Paul charges believers to flee idolatrous worship, and urges them not to turn the table of Christ the Master into the table of demons: "You cannot partake of the Lord's table and of the table of demons." He then commands them: "Whether you eat or drink, or whatever you do, do all to the glory of God" (vv. 10:21, 31).

The Catholic Epistle 1 Peter 1:2–8

Blessing God for salvation through Christ Jesus: Here, Peter blesses God, "who according to His abundant mercy has begotten us again to a living hope through the resurrection of Jesus Christ from the dead, to an inheritance incorruptible and undefiled and that does not fade away." Then, he urges believers to rejoice in this salvation, even if it requires them to be temporarily grieved by various trials (vv. 3–4).

The Acts Acts 21:5–14

Readiness to die for the faith: This passage shows that after the failed attempts of the disciples at Tyre to convince Paul not to go to Jerusalem, he and those with him went into the house of Philip the evangelist, where Agabus the prophet took Paul's belt and bound his own hands and feet signifying that the Jews will likewise bind the owner of this belt in Jerusalem, to which Paul answered: "I am ready not only to be bound, but also to die at Jerusalem for the name of the Lord Jesus" (v. 13).

FIFTH WEEK – FRIDAY
VENGEANCE OF THE FAITH
(Destruction coming upon unbelievers)

Linking the Readings:

All the readings of this day center on one theme: **Vengeance of the faith**—the destruction coming upon unbelievers

The first prophecy speaks of **God's restraints for believers**, as He commanded the Israelites of old when they enter the promised land to destroy its idols, to sacrifice in a specific place, and to refrain from eating blood; the second prophecy speaks of **proving the power of faith to them**, as Elijah proved it to the widow of Zarephath by raising her son from death; the third prophecy **warns them against strange gods and their worship** (what the Holy Bible refers to as harlotry), as the Sage warned in the Proverbs to keep away from the adulterous woman; the fourth prophecy speaks of **His promises to them**, as He promised through Isaiah to be with them so that no harm would come to them; and the fifth prophecy **warns them of self-righteousness**, as Elihu's anger was aroused against Job and his friends for relying on their self-righteousness.

In the Matins Gospel, the Savior **promises them His kingdom if they keep His commandments**, as He told the scribe who admitted that the first commandment is to love God from all the heart: "You are not far from the kingdom of God." In the Liturgy Gospel, He warns them of the **condemnation of unbelievers**, as He warned the Jews, saying that if they do not believe in Him, they will die in their sins.

In the Pauline Epistle, Paul reveals to them that **God chastens believers to give them the peaceable fruit of righteousness**; in the Catholic Epistle, Peter **consoles sufferers**, beseeching those who suffer to "commit their souls to Him in doing good, as to a faithful Creator";

and the Acts reading exhorts shepherds to always **visit their flock**, as Paul and Barnabas had decided.

PROPHECIES

First Prophecy — Deuteronomy 11:29–12:27

God's restraints for believers: In this passage, God commands His people, Israel, (as they are about to enter the promised land) that when they are established there to carefully observe to destroy its idols, carry their burnt offerings and sacrifices to the place He chooses for them, refrain from eating blood, and to not forsake the Levites all the days of their lives.

Second Prophecy — 1 Kings 17:2–24

Proving the power of faith to them: First, this passage shows that after Elijah prophesied against Ahab (who did evil in the sight of the Lord) that there would be no dew or rain in his land, the divine command came for him to go hide by the Brook Cherith (which flows into the Jordan), where ravens cared for him. Next, it shows how Elijah blessed the bin of flour and the jar of oil of the widow of Zarephath. Finally, it recounts the miracle Elijah did in raising the widow's son from death, causing her to cry: "Now by this I know that you are a man of God, and that the word of the Lord in your mouth is the truth" (v. 24).

Third Prophecy — Proverbs 5:1–12

Warning against strange gods and their worship: In this passage, the Sage commands his son to avoid the strange woman (symbolic of strange gods): "Remove your way far from her, and do not go near the door of her house, lest you give your honor to others, and your years to the cruel one." Doubtless the warning against harlotry is symbolic of not worshipping strange gods[27] (vv. 8–9).

Fourth Prophecy Isaiah 43:1–9

His promises to them: In this prophecy, God consoles the children of Israel with His promises to them (to be with them so that no harm would come to them): "When you pass through the waters, I will be with you; and through the rivers, they shall not overflow you." Continuing His promise, He says, "I will bring your descendants from the east, and gather you from the west; I will say to the north, 'Give them up!' And to the south, 'Do not keep them back!'" (vv. 2, 5–6).

Fifth Prophecy Job 30:9–32:5

Warning them of self-righteousness: In this passage, Job recounted his hardships and his goodness to his three friends, who ceased answering him "because he was righteous in his own eyes," so Elihu's anger was aroused against Job "because he justified himself rather than God," and against his three friends "because they had found no answer, and yet had condemned Job" (vv. 32:1–3).

---

[27] In many places, the Holy Bible calls the worship of strange idols harlotry: God commands the children of Israel not to give their sons in marriage to daughters who worship strange gods, so they do not "make your sons play the harlot with their gods" (Exodus 34:16); He commands them to offer their sacrifices at the door of the tabernacle, not offering them "to demons, after whom they have played the harlot" (Leviticus 17:7); and He complains about them when they worshipped strange gods during the days of the judges: "They would not listen to their judges, but they played the harlot with other gods, and bowed down to them" (Judges 2:17).

PSALMS AND GOSPELS

Matins Psalm — Psalms 86:9–10[28]

This psalm alludes to the accompanying gospel passage in which the scribe confesses that the first commandment is for people to love God from the whole heart, and thus urges people to worship Him: "All nations whom You have made shall come and worship before You, O Lord, and shall glorify Your name. For You are great, and do wondrous things; You alone are God."

Matins Gospel — Mark 12:28–34

In this passage, the Savior promises believers His Kingdom, as He responded to the one who answered that loving God from the whole heart is the first great commandment: "You are not far from the kingdom of God" (v. 34).

Liturgy Psalm — Psalms 138:1–2

This psalm alludes to the accompanying gospel passage in which the Savior threatens unbelievers with death, and on the tongue of believers confesses God's Lordship: "I will give thee thanks, O Lord, with my whole heart; and I will sing psalms to thee before the angels for You have heard all the words of my mouth. I will worship toward Your holy temple" (LXA Ps 138:1).[29]

---

[28] [In the Arabic book, these numbers are mistakenly entered as 8–9.]

[29] Here, the Septuagint (LXA–Brenton LXX with Apocrypha) version was used because NKJ and several other versions say "before the gods," although the Coptic text and the Greek translation say "before the angels."

Liturgy Gospel John 8:21–27

In this passage, the Savior warns of the condemnation of unbelievers, as He told the Jews: "If you do not believe that I am He, you will die in your sins" (v. 24).

EPISTLES

The Pauline Epistle Hebrews 12:5–16

God chastens believers: In this epistle, St Paul shows believers that as children, they should expect chastening: "For whom the Lord loves He chastens, and scourges every son whom He receives," and then he commands them to endure it to reap benefit, clarifying that: "Now no chastening seems to be joyful for the present, but painful; nevertheless, afterward it yields the peaceable fruit of righteousness to those who have been trained by it" (vv. 6, 11).

The Catholic Epistle 1 Peter 4:15–5:5

Consoling them during suffering: Here, Peter consoles those who are suffering: "Let those who suffer according to the will of God commit their souls to Him in doing good, as to a faithful Creator," then he commissions priests to shepherd the flock of God, for the sake of "the crown of glory that does not fade away" (vv. 4:19; 5:4).

The Acts Acts 15:36–16:3

Visiting the flock: In this passage, Paul exhorts shepherds to the importance of visiting the brethren everywhere (imitating Saints Paul and Barnabas), as Paul told Barnabas: "Let us now go back and visit our brethren in every city where we have preached the word of the

Lord, and see how they are doing." Barnabas took Mark and traveled to Cyprus, while Paul chose Silas and, going to Derbe and Lystra, he found Timothy, whom he took as a disciple.

FIFTH WEEK – SATURDAY
GUIDANCE OF THE FAITH

Linking the Readings:

All the readings of this day center on one theme: **Guidance of the faith**—guiding believers against straying into sin from the way of life

The Matins Gospel speaks of the **Savior's joy over accepting the penance of the repentant**, as the owner rejoiced over the return of the lost sheep and the woman rejoiced in finding the lost coin. The Liturgy Gospel speaks of **Him seeking to guide sinners**, as the Lord of glory tried to gather to Himself the children of Jerusalem "as a hen gathers her chicks under her wings, but they were not willing."

In the Pauline Epistle, Paul urges believers to **restore brethren who fall into trespasses in a spirit of gentleness**; in the Catholic Epistle, James commands them to **endure any sufferings they encounter**; and the Acts reading reveals **the need to guide Gentiles also** as Paul was sent to them for this very purpose.

PSALMS AND GOSPELS

Matins Psalm — Psalms 65:2–3

This psalm points to the acceptance of sinners who repent (as the returned lost sheep and the found coin mentioned in the Gospel passage) and on their behalf, it entreats God to accept their repentance: "O You who hear prayer, to You all flesh will come. Iniquities prevail against me."

Matins Gospel Luke 15:3–10

This passage shows that the Savior rejoices in accepting the penance of the repentant sinner [as the owner rejoiced over the return of the lost sheep, and the woman rejoiced in finding the lost coin], as He told the tax collectors and sinners who were listening to Him: "Likewise, I say to you, there is joy in the presence of the angels of God over one sinner who repents" (v. 10).

Liturgy Psalm Psalms 143:1–2

The second part of the psalm points to the judgment of Jerusalem, which will be destroyed for rejecting the faith. And speaking for the believers led by faith, it asks God to answer their supplications, and forgive them: "Hear my prayer, O Lord, give ear to my supplications! In Your faithfulness answer me, and in Your righteousness. Do not enter into judgment with Your servant."

Liturgy Gospel Matthew 23:13–39

This passage shows that the Savior seeks to guide sinners to the faith, as He said (after pronouncing woes on the scribes and Pharisees): "O Jerusalem, Jerusalem, the one who kills the prophets and stones those who are sent to her! How often I wanted to gather your children together, as a hen gathers her chicks under her wings, but you were not willing" (v. 37).

EPISTLES

The Pauline Epistle Galatians 5:16–6:2

Restoring brethren who trespass: At the start of this epistle, Paul commands believers to walk in the Spirit, not fulfilling the lust of the flesh, "For the flesh lusts against the Spirit, and the Spirit against the flesh." He then lists the works of the flesh and the fruit of the Spirit, finally asking them to restore anyone who trespasses: "Brethren, if a man is overtaken in any trespass, you who are spiritual restore such a one in a spirit of gentleness, considering yourself lest you also be tempted" (vv. 5:17; 6:1).

The Catholic Epistle James 5:7–11

Enduring any sufferings they encounter: Here, James charges them to endure the temptations or hardships that come upon them, imitating Job and the prophets: "My brethren, take the prophets, who spoke in the name of the Lord, as an example of suffering and patience. Indeed we count them blessed who endure. You have heard of the perseverance of Job and seen the end intended by the Lord" (vv. 10–11).

The Acts Acts 26:1–18

Needing to guide Gentiles also: This passage shows that guidance should not be restricted to sinning believers only, but should extend to Gentiles. As Paul stood before King Agrippa defending himself, he recounted his life story from his youth, and how he was called to the apostleship as God said to him: "But rise and stand on your feet; for I have appeared to you for this purpose, to make you a minister and a witness both of the things which you have seen and of the things which I will yet reveal to you. I will deliver you from the Jewish people, as well as from the Gentiles, to whom I now send you, to open their eyes, in order to turn them from darkness to light, and from the power of Satan to God, that they may receive forgiveness of sins and an inheritance among those who are sanctified by faith in Me" (v. 16–18).

FIFTH WEEK – SUNDAY
STRENGTHENING THE FAITH[30]

Linking the Readings:

All the readings of this day center on one theme: **Strengthening the faith**—the strength of faith that empowers believers' spirituality

In the Vespers Gospel, the Savior promises to **avenge those who cry out to Him**, as the unjust judge avenged the widow; in the Matins Gospel, He **promises them His kingdom**, as He took the vineyard from the wicked vinedressers and gave it to others who will render to Him its fruit in due season; in the Liturgy Gospel, He reveals that He will **strengthen believers' spiritual vigor**, as He strengthened the joints of the infirm man who lay at the pool of Bethesda for thirty-eight years and he was healed, carried his bed, and walked; and in the Evening Gospel, He **forgives their sins**, as He forgave the paralytic who was let down from the ceiling and healed him.

In the Pauline Epistle, Paul urges **believers to stand fast in the faith during hardships**, as he urged the Thessalonians; in the Catholic Epistle, Peter exhorts them on the need to **be holy until Christ's Second Coming**; the Acts reading urges them to **endure prosecution for the faith**, as Paul endured before King Agrippa.

PSALMS AND GOSPELS

Vespers Psalm — Psalm 39:12

This psalm alludes to the accompanying gospel passage in which the widow asks for vengeance from the unjust judge, with this widow symbolic of the tormented soul enslaved to bodily lusts and evil

[30] This Sunday is known as Infirm Man Sunday.

thoughts but finds no succorer. The psalm cries out with her to God for rescue: "Hear my prayer, O Lord, and give ear to my cry; do not be silent at my tears; for I am a stranger with You, a sojourner, as all my fathers were."

Vespers Gospel Luke 18:1–8

This passage shows that the Savior avenges believers who cry out to Him from their enslavement to lusts, as He said in the parable of the widow and the unjust judge: "Shall God not avenge His own elect who cry out day and night to Him, though He bears long with them? I tell you that He will avenge them speedily" (vv. 7–8).

Matins Psalm Psalms 102:1–2, 12

This psalm alludes to the parable of the wicked vinedressers, mentioned in the accompanying gospel passage, and speaking for the believers who fear the kingdom being taken away because of their sins and having it given to a nation rendering its fruits, the psalm begs God to hear their prayers and confesses His kingdom's perpetuity: "Hear my prayer, O Lord, and let my cry come to You. Do not hide Your face from me. But You, O Lord, shall endure forever, and the remembrance of Your name to all generations."

Matins Gospel Matthew 21:33–46

This passage speaks of the Savior's kingdom being granted to righteous believers, as He told the chief priests and Pharisees in the parable of the vineyard and vinedressers: "Therefore I say to you, the kingdom of God will be taken from you and given to a nation bearing the fruits of it" (v. 43).

Liturgy Psalm Psalms 33:5–6

This psalm points to the accompanying gospel passage, in which God had mercy on the infirm man laid by the pool of Bethesda and gave power for his legs to be strengthened, after which he stood up, carried his bed, and walked: "He loves mercy and judgment; the earth is full of the Lord's mercy. By the word of the Lord the heavens were established, and all the hosts of them by the breath of his mouth."[31]

Liturgy Gospel John 5:1–18

This passage shows that the Savior spiritually strengthens believers, as He told the infirm man, "'Rise, take up your bed and walk.' And immediately the man was made well, took up his bed, and walked" (vv. 8–9).

Evening Psalm Psalms 142:1–2

This psalm alludes to the accompanying gospel passage in which the paralytic let down from the ceiling was forgiven his sins (the cause of his illness), and speaking for sinners, it asks God to forgive them: "I cry out to the Lord with my voice; with my voice to the Lord I make my supplication. I pour out my complaint before Him; I declare before Him my trouble."

Evening Gospel Matthew 9:1–8

This passage shows that the Savior forgives the believers' sins, as He told the paralytic: "Son, be of good cheer; your sins are forgiven you" (v. 2).

---

[31] SAAS (Saint Athanasius Academy Septuagint) was used for accuracy.

EPISTLES

The Pauline Epistle — 2 Thessalonians 2:1–17

Believers stand fast in the faith during hardships: In this epistle, Paul charges believers to remain steadfast in the truth they received (showing them that a day will come in which many will apostatize the faith, accompanied by the appearance of the Antichrist—before Christ's second coming), and therefore says: "Therefore, brethren, stand fast and hold the traditions which you were taught, whether by word or our epistle" (v. 15).

The Catholic Epistle — 2 Peter 3:1–18

Be holy until Christ's Second Coming: Here, Peter affirms the certainty of Christ the Master's Second Coming (refuting the scoffing antagonists' opinions), warns them against postponing or delaying repentance, describes the end of the world, and charges them as they await this Coming to pursue holiness: "Therefore, beloved, looking forward to these things, be diligent to be found by Him in peace, without spot and blameless; and consider that the longsuffering of our Lord is salvation" (vv. 14–15).

The Acts — Acts 26:19–27:8

Enduring prosecution for the faith: This passage shows that believers should endure even prosecution for the faith, as Paul stood as the accused before King Agrippa, and Festus charged him with madness, to which Paul responded politely. His defense drew Agrippa to his side and convinced all those present that he was not guilty, so Agrippa told Festus: "This man might have been set free if he had not appealed to Caesar." Finally, Paul and his friends began their journey to Rome (v. 26:32).

WEEK 5: GOAL OF THE STRUGGLE (FAITH)

DAY	*PROPHECIES*		PSALMS & GOSPELS: Matins	PSALMS & GOSPELS: Liturgy	*EPISTLES: Pauline*	*EPISTLES: Catholicon*	*EPISTLES: Acts*
MONDAY: RELIANCE ON FAITH	*1 **Prov**: Believers' reliance on God*	*2 **Is**: He gives them length of days*	The Savior ends the lives of those who rely on money	He satiates believers who rely on Him with Gospel nourishment	*Rejoicing over believers' unity and humility*	*Suffering for righteousness' sake (the faith)*	*Accepting Gentiles without partiality*
	*3 **Job**: His riches and honor await them*						
TUESDAY: FAITH-MINISTRY	*1 **Num**: Servants participate in faith-ministry*	*2 **Prov**: Faith-ministry grace*	The Savior reveals His mercy to the weak in faith	He personally ministers in the temple	*Faith-ministers' faithfulness*	*Loving one another*	*Defending the faith*
	*3 **Is**: Faith-ministry's endurance*			*4 **Job**: People's corruptness*		*5 **Job**: God's unfathomable power*	
WEDNESDAY: HOPE OF FAITH	*1 **Ex**: Believers' hope in God's might*	*2 **Is**: God's security to them*	The bond of faith of believers	His patience on believers who are yet to produce fruit	*Confidence in the hope of faith*	*Believers' consolation in Him*	*Gentiles gain salvation through Him*
	*3 **Joel**: God's blessings to them*	*4 **Job**: Urging them to live in wisdom*		*5 **Prov**: Avoiding the path of the wicked*		*6 **1 Sam**: Blessing their descendants*	
THURSDAY: FREEDOM OF FAITH	*1 **Is**: Him loosening the bonds of believers*	*2 **Prov**: Urging them to holiness*	The Savior exorcizes unclean spirits from them	He loosens the bonds of Satan from them	*Fleeing idolatrous worship*	*Blessing God for salvation through Christ Jesus*	*Readiness to die for the faith in the name of the Savior*
	*3 **Job**: Desiring their former spiritual glory*			*4 **1 Sam**: Empowering them spiritually*			
FRIDAY: VENGEANCE OF THE FAITH	*1 **Deut**: God's restraints for believers*	*2 **1 Kin**: Proving the power of faith*	The Savior promises believers His Kingdom	The Savior condemns unbelievers	*God chastens believers*	*Consoling them in suffering*	*Visiting the flock*
	*3 **Prov**: Warning against strange gods*		*4 **Is**: His promises to believers*		*5 **Job**: Warning of self-righteousness*		
SATURDAY: GUIDANCE OF THE FAITH			He rejoices in accepting the repentant	He seeks to guide sinners	*Restoring brethren who trespass*	*Enduring any sufferings they encounter*	*Needing to guide Gentiles also*
SUNDAY: STRENGTHENING THE FAITH	**Vespers Gospel** He avenges those who cry out to Him	**Matins Gospel** He promises them His Kingdom	**Liturgy Gospel** He strengthens believers' spiritually	**Evening Gospel** He forgives their sins	*Believers stand fast in the faith during hardships*	*Be holy until Christ's Second Coming*	*Enduring prosecution for the faith*

UNIVERSAL THEME:
ANOINTING OF THE STRUGGLE (BAPTISM)

SIXTH WEEK – MONDAY
REPENTANCE OF BAPTISM

Linking the Readings:

All the readings of this day center on one theme: **Repentance of baptism**—repentance that precedes baptism, typified in the rite of 'Renouncing Satan' during baptism

In the first prophecy, God **calls sinners to repentance**, as wisdom calls out to fools to receive instruction and have an understanding heart; in the second prophecy, **God promises to forgive their sins**, as He told Israel on the tongue of Isaiah, "I, even I, am He who blots out your transgressions"; and in the third prophecy, He promises to **give them understanding**, as Elihu revealed to Job and his friends: "There is a spirit in man, and the breath of the Almighty gives him understanding."

In the Matins Gospel, He promises to **destroy their wicked negligent shepherds**, as He destroyed the wicked vinedressers and gave the vineyard to others; and in the Liturgy Gospel He **urges them to repent, lest they perish**, as He warned the Jews of their destruction if they do not repent.

In the Pauline Epistle, Paul commands them to **walk properly**, as he commanded the Thessalonians; in the Catholic Epistle, James stirs them to **being humble and non-judgmental**; and the Acts reading confirms their **objectors' failed attempts**, as Gallio refused to listen to the Jews when they presented their complaints against Paul.

PROPHECIES

First Prophecy — Proverbs 8:1–11

Calling sinners to repentance: In this passage, Wisdom calls sinners to return from their foolishness: "O you simple ones, understand prudence, and you fools, be of an understanding heart," further clarifying her call: "Receive my instruction, and not silver, and knowledge rather than choice gold" (vv. 5, 10).

Second Prophecy — Isaiah 43:10–28

God promises to forgive their sins: Here, God calls the people of Israel to witness the works of His might, revealing to them the destruction coming upon wicked Babylon, and His amazing salvation for His people. Then, He rebukes them for short-changing Him on what is rightfully His, and promises them forgiveness: "I, even I, am He who blots out your transgressions for My own sake; and I will not remember your sins" (v. 25).

Third Prophecy — Job 32:6–16

Giving them understanding: This passage shows how Elihu's wrath was kindled against Job (because he considered himself more righteous than God) and against his friends (because although they were unable to answer Job they still condemned him). Despite his youth, he displayed that wisdom is not always with age, declaring, "There is a spirit in man, and the breath of the Almighty gives him understanding." He dismisses his youthfulness and rebukes the three friends for not answering Job, standing firm in his opinion (v. 8).

PSALMS AND GOSPELS

Matins Psalm — Psalm 38:9

Speaking for the believers who were neglected by the shepherds (alluding to the accompanying gospel passage in which the wicked vinedressers neglected the vineyard), this psalm presents their desires and the condition of their sufferings: "Lord, all my desire is before You; and my sighing is not hidden from You."

Matins Gospel — Mark 12:1–12

This passage speaks of the Savior destroying the wicked shepherds (that is, negligent guardians), as He told the chief priests, Pharisees, and the elders in the parable of the vineyard: "Therefore what will the owner of the vineyard do? He will come and destroy the vinedressers, and give the vineyard to others" (v. 9).

Liturgy Psalm — Psalms 35:1–2

Speaking for believers battled by evil forces that prevent them from repentance (as Pilate slew the Galileans mentioned in the accompanying gospel passage), this psalm asks God to come to their rescue in their spiritual warfare: "Plead my cause, O Lord, with those who strive with me; fight against those who fight against me. Take hold of shield and buckler, and stand up for my help."

Liturgy Gospel — Luke 13:1–5

In this passage, the Savior urges believers to repent, as He told the Jews, "Unless you repent you will all likewise perish" (v.5).

EPISTLES

The Pauline Epistle — 1 Thessalonians 4:1–18

Walking properly: In this epistle, Paul commands believers to walk properly so as to please God, highlighting the main points on this path: abstaining from sexual immorality, engaging in brotherly love, and not mourning over the departed "as others who have no hope" (v. 13).

The Catholic Epistle — James 4:7–12

Being humble and non-judgmental: Here, James advises them to be arrayed in humility: "Humble yourselves in the sight of the Lord, and He will lift you up," which will lead them to stop judging others (v. 10).

The Acts — Acts 18:9–18

Objectors' failed attempts: This passage mentions how God appeared to Paul in a vision by night to encourage him to continue the mission, promising him that no one would harm him. This was manifest when the Jews complained to Gallio that Paul persuades people to worship God contrary to the law; Gallio refused to listen to them and dismissed them.

SIXTH WEEK – TUESDAY
CONFESSION OF BAPTISM

Linking the Readings:

All the readings of this day center on one theme: **Confession of baptism**—the confession of faith that follows 'Renouncing Satan' and precedes baptism

The first prophecy speaks of **urging believers to confess their faith**, as wisdom [faith] promises those who seek her with wealth and honor; the second prophecy speaks of **God's comfort to those who confess Him**, as He promised the Israelites through Isaiah that He will pour His water on the thirsty and His Spirit on their descendants; the third prophecy speaks of the **delegates ransoming them**, as Elihu told Job that God "will redeem his soul from going down to the Pit"; and the fourth prophecy speaks of this **ransom being free**, as Namaan the Syrian was ransomed freely of his leprosy at the hands of Elisha, whose servant Gehazi was punished for taking compensation.

The Matins Gospel speaks of **believers who confess their faith being rejected in their own country**, as the Savior was rejected in His own country when people attested to Him for the words of grace coming out of His mouth. The Liturgy Gospel exhorts them to **confess their faith**, as becomes clear from Peter's confession in answer to Christ the Master's question.

In the Pauline Epistle, Paul **urges believers to prophesy** so that others attest that God truly is among them; in the Catholic Epistle, James speaks of the need to **combine their faith with works**; and the Acts reading reveals that the **power of faith performs wonders and prevails over magic**, as the apostles worked wonders, and magic went up in smoke before the might of Paul.

PROPHECIES

First Prophecy Proverbs 8:12–21

Urging believers to confess their faith: In this prophecy, wisdom (symbolic of confession of faith) cries out concerning the wealth and honor awaiting those who love her: "Riches and honor are with me, enduring riches and righteousness... That I may cause those who love me to inherit wealth, that I may fill their treasuries" (vv. 18, 21).

Second Prophecy Isaiah 44:1–8

God's comfort to confessors: This prophecy speaks of the comfort that God provides to those who confess their faith because in it, God tells His people through Isaiah: "Fear not, O Jacob My servant... For I will pour water on him who is thirsty, and floods on the dry ground; I will pour My Spirit on your descendants, and My blessing on your offspring" (vv. 2–3).

Third Prophecy Job 32:17–33:33

Delegates ransom them: In this passage, Elihu revealed his opinion when Job's friends could not answer Job, who declared his self-righteousness. Before presenting evidence for his opinion, he, as a delegate for God, answers Job in meekness and uprightness of heart—justifying the excellent wisdom of God who does not reveal His ways to humans. He proceeds to declare his opinion that God calls man to repentance by visions of night, by pains in his sleep, and by a messenger who intercedes for him, mediating thus: "Deliver him from going down to the Pit; I have found a ransom," at which point this person sings: "'I have sinned, and perverted what was right, and it did not profit me.' He will redeem his soul from going down to the Pit, and his life shall see the light" (v. 33:24, 27–28).

Fourth Prophecy 2 Kings 5:1–27[32]

Free ransom: This prophecy completes the meaning of the previous one, as Elisha healed Namaan the Syrian of his leprosy (symbolic of sin), to which he responded: "Indeed, now I know that there is no God in all the earth, except in Israel." Elisha refused to take the gifts Namaan offered for his healing, yet the leprosy clung to Gehazi (Elisha's servant) and his descendants forever as penalty for slandering his master's name by taking the gifts; the gifts of God cannot be sold for money (v. 15).

PSALMS AND GOSPELS

Matins Psalm Psalm 35:13

Speaking for those confessing their faith and who are humbled before God in fasts, begging His mercy, as did the widow of Zarephath and Namaan the Syrian who were aware of this mercy (mentioned in the accompanying gospel passage), this psalm cries out to God: "My clothing was sackcloth; I humbled myself with fasting; and my prayer would return to my own heart."

Matins Gospel Luke 4:22–30

In this passage, the Savior is rejected as a prophet in His own country, as shown when He told the people of Nazareth: "Assuredly, I say to you, no prophet is accepted in his own country" (v. 24).

---

[32] This prophecy was removed in the new Katameros without justification, as it completes the meaning.

Liturgy Psalm Psalm 42:1

Speaking for those longing to come to God (to confess their faith in Him), this psalm says: "As the deer pants for the water brooks, so pants my soul for You, O God."

Liturgy Gospel Luke 9:18–22

In this passage, the Savior urges His disciples to confess their faith, saying, "'But who do you say that I am?' Peter answered and said, 'The Christ of God'" (v. 20).

EPISTLES

The Pauline Epistle 1 Corinthians 14:18–28

Urging believers to prophesy: In this epistle, Paul shows that tongues are a sign to unbelievers, but prophecy is for believers. Based on this, Paul urges them to prophesy and openly confess the faith: "But if all prophesy, and an unbeliever or an uninformed person comes in, he is convinced by all... and so, falling down on his face, he will worship God and report that God is truly among you" (vv. 24–25).

The Catholic Epistle James 1:22–2:1

Being doers of the word: Here, James urges those who confess their faith to be doers of the word, not only hearers, noting: "But he who looks into the perfect law of liberty and continues in it, and is not a forgetful hearer but a doer of the work, this one will be blessed in what he does" (v. 25).

The Acts Acts 19:11–20

Prevailing over magic: As for this passage, it shows that signs follow believers, and the power of faith expels evil spirits and prevails over magic, as seen with the magicians after the man in whom was an evil spirit overpowered the itinerant Jewish exorcists: "Many of those who had practiced magic brought their books together and burned them in the sight of all" (v. 19).

SIXTH WEEK – WEDNESDAY
JUDGMENT OF BAPTISM

Linking the Readings:

All the readings of this day center on one theme: **The judgment of baptism**—judging 'godparents' (or more generally shepherds) who neglect their pledge to care for their 'godchildren's' upbringing in Christ the Master's laws as they vowed during baptism

The first prophecy speaks of **God threatening to punish unjust shepherds**, as He threatened Pharaoh (after the locust and darkness plagues) with the tenth plague of killing the firstborn. The second prophecy speaks of Him **redeeming His faithful people**, as He told Israel on the tongue of Isaiah, "Return to Me, for I have redeemed you." The third prophecy speaks of **quickening them**, as wisdom blesses whoever listens to her watchfully, promising life and favor from the Lord. The fourth prophecy speaks of **submitting to Him**, as Job humbled himself before God and said, "If I have done iniquity, I will do no more." The fifth prophecy speaks of **their honor**, as Jesus the son of Sirach commanded, "Keep thy soul in meekness, and give it honor according to its desert."

The Matins Gospel speaks of the Savior **reprimanding hypocritical shepherds**, as He reproached the Pharisees who honor God with their lips while their hearts are far away from Him; while the Liturgy Gospel speaks of the Savior **condemning them**, as He condemned the Pharisees and lawyers for bringing upon them all the blood of the prophets shed on the earth, from the blood of righteous Abel to the blood of Zechariah the son of Berechiah.

The Pauline Epistle speaks of the **judgment of negligent hypocritical shepherds**, as the apostle proved this by saying that all the shepherds who have sinned in the law will be judged by the law, whether Gentiles or Jews; the Catholic Epistle reveals that **their destruction is**

swift, as Peter admitted in his second epistle that "their judgment has not been idle, and their destruction does not slumber"; and the Acts reading speaks of **confronting them**, as Paul objected to the false accusations by the Jews against him before King Agrippa.

PROPHECIES

First Prophecy — Exodus 10:1–11:10

God threatens to punish unjust shepherds: This prophecy tells of the plagues of locust and darkness that came upon Pharaoh, yet God hardened his heart so that he would not let the children of Israel go. Furthermore, it reveals that although God threatened him with the tenth and final plague—killing the firstborn—his heart remained hardened against letting the children of Israel leave his land.

Second Prophecy — Isaiah 44:21–28

Redeeming His faithful people: In this prophecy, God calls out to Israel through Isaiah to return to Him because He has redeemed them. For this, Isaiah urges them to praise Him: "Break forth into singing, you mountains, O forest, and every tree in it! For the Lord has redeemed Jacob, and glorified Himself in Israel," and for His greatness in single-handedly stretching out the heavens and spreading out the earth (v. 23).

Third Prophecy — Proverbs 8:22–36

Quickening them: In this passage, Wisdom speaks of her eternity, calling the children to keep her ways and promising them life: "Blessed is the man who listens to me, watching daily... For whoever finds me finds life, and obtains favor from the Lord" (vv. 34–35).

Fourth Prophecy | Job 34:1–37

Submitting to Him: Here, Elihu charges Job of attributing injustice to God, showing him that God, by virtue of His greatness, cannot be unjust. Next, he commands Job to admit submission to His will, by confessing: "Teach me what I do not see; if I have done iniquity, I will do no more" (v. 32).

Fifth Prophecy | Sirach 10:1–31[33]

Their honor: Completing the meaning of the previous prophecy, the son of Sirach shows that the Lord will wipe out the memory of the proud and retain the memory of the humble, showing that they would be honored in His sight: "In the midst of brethren their chief is honorable: so shall they that fear the Lord, be in his eyes," and calling them to glorify their souls: "My son, keep thy soul in meekness, and give it honor according to its desert" (DRA Sir 10: 20(24), 28(31)).[34]

PSALMS AND GOSPELS

Matins Psalm | Psalms 102:17, 20

While the accompanying Gospel draws attention to those worshipping God with their lips and not their heart, the psalm urges heart-worshippers (the destitute) to praise the Lord for answering their request: "He shall regard the prayer of the destitute, and shall

[33] This prophecy was removed in the new Katameros without justification, as it completes the meaning.
[34] Here the Douay-Rheims American Edition (DRA–1899) is the closest to the Coptic text.

not despise their prayer. To declare the name of the Lord in Zion, and His praise in Jerusalem."

Matins Gospel Mark 7:1–20

In this passage, the Savior reprimands those who worship Him with their lips and not their hearts, as He rebuked the scribes and Pharisees who derided his disciples for eating with unwashed hands (although what defiles a person is what comes out—evil thoughts—and not the food that enters the mouth). The Lord described them with the saying of Isaiah: "This people honors Me with their lips, but their heart is far from Me" (v. 6).

Liturgy Psalm Psalms 9:11–12

While the second part of this psalm alludes to the accompanying gospel passage in which the Lord requires of the Jews the blood of the prophets shed from the foundation of the world, the first part charges believers to praise Him for this just decree and declare His works before the nations: "Sing praises to the Lord, who dwells in Zion! Declare His deeds among the people. When He avenges blood, He remembers them."

Liturgy Gospel Luke 11:45–52

In this passage, the Savior condemns hypocritical shepherds (an example of negligent godparents) because they demand godliness but their works contradict their words. As proof of His judgment, He said of the lawyers: "I will send them prophets and apostles, and some of them they will kill and persecute, that the blood of all the prophets which was shed from the foundation of the world may be required of this generation" (vv. 49–50).

EPISTLES

The Pauline Epistle — Romans 2:12–24

Judging hypocritical shepherds: In this passage, the apostle shows that those who sin (whether Gentiles or Jews), even if they are appointed to judge other people's sins, will not be saved from God's condemnation. Paul tells them explicitly: "You who make your boast in the law, do you dishonor God through breaking the law? For 'the name of God is blasphemed among the Gentiles because of you,' as it is written" (vv. 23–24).

The Catholic Epistle — 2 Peter 1:20–2:6

Their destruction is swift: After exhorting believers to stand firm in their faith in Christ the Master as the Son of God, according to the testimony of the apostles who were eyewitnesses to His glory, and according to the Father's own testimony, and the testimony of the prophets (mentioned in the preface to this passage), Peter proceeds to foretell the coming of false teachers—declaring their harlotry and retribution, and that of their followers: "For a long time their judgment has not been idle, and their destruction does not slumber," giving examples of the angels who sinned, Noah's era, and the people of Sodom and Gomorrah (v. 3).

The Acts — Acts 26:1–8

Confronting them: In this passage, Paul confronts the false charges laid against him before King Agrippa by the Jews, clarifying how he lived his whole life a Pharisee according to the strictest sect of their religion, showing his surprise at being brought to court for this cause.

SIXTH WEEK – THURSDAY
LIFE OF BAPTISM

Linking the Readings:

All the readings of this day center on one theme: **The life of baptism**—the eternal life gained by the baptized who have faithful godparents (shepherds) who care to feed them the bread of life

The first prophecy speaks of **shepherds quickening believers**, as Elisha revived first the son of the Shunammite woman and later the sons of the prophets who ate of the poisonous wild gourds. The second prophecy speaks of **God supporting the shepherds for the believers' sake**, as He supported Cyrus (his anointed) for the sake of His servant Jacob and His people Israel. The third prophecy speaks of **Him prolonging their lives**, as wisdom calls out that in gaining her, one's days are prolonged. The fourth prophecy speaks of **Him answering their petitions**, as Elihu told Job that God listens, but not to the wicked. The fifth prophecy speaks of **His commandments to them**, as divine inspiration commands in Ecclesiasticus (Wisdom of Jesus the son of Sirach) to attain wisdom and not judge others.

The Matins Gospel reveals that **the Savior destroys wicked shepherds**, as He affirmed in the parable of the vineyard and the wicked vinedressers, giving the vineyard to others; while the Liturgy Gospel speaks of **Him giving believers life**, as He said with His pure mouth that whoever eats His flesh and drinks His blood has eternal life.

In the Pauline Epistle, Paul **urges believers to godliness**, commanding the men to lift up holy hands; the women to continue in faith, love, holiness, and propriety; and the bishops to have their children in submission with all reverence. In the Catholic Epistle, Jude commands them to also be **concerned for the salvation of others**; and the Acts reading speaks of their **exposure to dangers**, as Paul and his companions faced the vehement sea storm.

PROPHECIES

First Prophecy 2 Kings 4:8–41[35]

Shepherds quicken believers: This prophecy tells how the woman of Shunem hosted Elisha, and he returned the favor by prophesying the birth of her son, and when this son died Elisha restored him to life. Later, his servant cooked wild gourds (unknowingly gathered by one of the sons of the prophets) for the sons of the prophets during the famine. When they ate, they said, "there is death in the pot," so Elisha asked for flour from his servant and put it into the pot, and they all ate without any harm.

Second Prophecy Isaiah 45:1–10

God supports shepherds for the believers' sake: In this prophecy, the Lord announced His support to Cyrus (his anointed), for the sake of His servant Jacob: "I will go before you... I will give you the treasures of darkness and hidden riches of secret places... For Jacob My servant's sake, and Israel My elect, I have even called you by your name" (vv. 2–4).

Third Prophecy Proverbs 9:1–11

Prolonging their lives: Here, Wisdom cries out, "Come, eat of my bread and drink of the wine I have mixed." After showing that "the fear of the Lord is the beginning of wisdom," she advises those who are attaining to wisdom: "For by me your days will be multiplied, and years of life will be added to you" (vv. 5, 10–11).

---

[35] This reading only goes to verse 37 according to the new Katameros.

Fourth Prophecy Job 35:1–16

Answering their petitions: In this passage, Elihu addresses Job who accused God of injustice, clarifying that he has no right to say that he is more righteous than God, as our goodness or wickedness cannot affect the Almighty. He adds that many cry out to Him in their troubles, yet He does not hear those who lack faith: "Surely God will not listen to empty talk, nor will the Almighty regard it" (v. 13).

Fifth Prophecy Sirach 11:1–10[36]

His commandments to them: This prophecy shows that the meek person's wisdom exalts his head and seats him with the notables; then it instructs believers not to make a quick judgment before investigating, and not to meddle in many matters: "If you multiply activities, you will not be held blameless" (v. 10[37]).

PSALMS AND GOSPELS

Matins Psalm Psalm 9:13

Speaking for believers who fall prey to wicked shepherds (such as the vinedressers who neglected the vineyard so that it produced no grapes, mentioned in the accompanying gospel passage), this psalm asks God to rescue them from the oppression of those wicked shepherds and from the spiritual death that has overpowered them, then it begs mercy: "Have mercy on me, O Lord! Consider my trouble from those who hate me, You who lift me up from the gates of death."

---

[36] This prophecy was removed in the new Katameros, without justification, as it completes the meaning.

[37] New Revised Standard Version was used for compatibility with the Coptic text.

Matins Gospel Luke 20:9–19

This passage speaks of the Savior destroying wicked shepherds, as He advised the chief priests, scribes, and elders that the owner of the vineyard "will come and destroy those vinedressers and give the vineyard to others" (v. 16).

Liturgy Psalm Psalms 9:13–14

Speaking for believers whose souls live on spiritual nourishment offered by faithful shepherds (explained as Christ the Master's body and blood in the accompanying gospel passage), this psalm praises God: "You who lift me up from the gates of death, that I may tell of all Your praise in the gates of the daughter of Zion."

Liturgy Gospel John 6:47–71

This passage speaks of the Savior giving life to believers—those whose shepherds take care to nourish with spiritual food (His Holy body and blood), as He said: "Whoever eats My flesh and drinks My blood has eternal life, and I will raise him up at the last day" (v. 54).

EPISTLES

The Pauline Epistle 1 Timothy 2:1–3:4

Urging believers to godliness: In this passage, the apostle, as a faithful shepherd, addresses his flock (the men and women, and their shepherds the bishops) urging them to godliness. He advises: a) men to "pray everywhere, lifting up holy hands, without wrath and doubting," b) women to "adorn themselves in modest apparel, with propriety and moderation... which is proper for women professing godliness, with good works," and c) the capable teaching bishop to be "one who rules his own house well, having his children in submission with all reverence" (vv. 2:8, 9–10; 3:4).

The Catholic Epistle Jude 1:16–25

Concern for the salvation of others: Here, Jude urges believers to be concerned not only for themselves, but also for others: "And on some have compassion, making a distinction; but others save with fear, pulling them out of the fire, hating even the garment defiled by the flesh" (v. 22–23).

The Acts Acts 27:16–20

Exposure to dangers: This passage shows that believers will encounter difficulties in their mission, as Paul and his companions were exposed to dangers when the sea storm was vehement against them: "Now when neither sun nor stars appeared for many days, and no small tempest beat on us, all hope that we would be saved was finally given up" (v. 20).

SIXTH WEEK – FRIDAY
RESURRECTION OF BAPTISM

Linking the Readings:

All the readings of this day center on one theme: **The resurrection of baptism**—resurrecting the baptized from the death of sin, typified by immersing the baby in the baptismal font and raising the baby from it again. Baptism is symbolic of the mystery of Christ the Master's death and resurrection, as Paul attests that we "were baptized into His death" (Romans 6:3). Through baptism, the baptized is reborn, and the ancestral sin and previous sins are washed away, therefore, the Master said, "Most assuredly, I say to you, unless one is born of water and the Spirit, he cannot enter the kingdom of God."

The first prophecy speaks of **God resurrecting the baptized**, as Isaac was redeemed by the ram (his slaughter was symbolic of the Savior's death), being slaughtered by intention, and returning alive as Christ the Master died and rose. Since baptism is symbolic of the mystery of Christ's death and resurrection, Isaac's slaughter here is symbolic of baptism in which the babe is buried and snatched, purified from sin. The second prophecy speaks of **His salvation for believers**-salvation based on baptism, as Isaiah claims: "Israel shall be saved by the Lord with an everlasting salvation." The third prophecy speaks of **Him warning them against sinning after baptism**, as the Sage warned in Proverbs of the foolish woman who entices passersby, to whom the naïve incline. In the fourth prophecy, **He urges them to magnify His works**, as Elihu commands Job to magnify God's works. The fifth prophecy speaks of **them fearing Him**, as Elihu thus commanded Job after mentioning to him God's unfathomable power. The sixth prophecy speaks of **Him saving them**, as Tobias was rescued from death.

The Matins Gospel speaks of **the Savior pardoning or clearing the baptized**, as He said that whoever believes in Him will not be condemned; while the Liturgy Gospel **urges them to baptism**, as He determined that whoever is not born of the water and Spirit cannot enter the kingdom of God.

In the Pauline Epistle, Paul **warns the baptized against relapsing into sin after baptism**, declaring, "Therefore let him who thinks he stands take heed lest he fall." In the Catholic Epistle, John exhorts them **not to love the world**, as he says, "Do not love the world or the things in the world." The Acts reading speaks of **receiving the Holy Spirit after baptism**, as Peter and John placed their hands on the Samaritans who believed and so they received the Holy Spirit.

PROPHECIES

First Prophecy — Genesis 22:1–18

Resurrecting the baptized: This prophecy shows that God tested Abraham, asking him to offer his son as a burnt sacrifice on one of the mountains. Abraham revealed his faith and obedience, at which point the angel prevented him from harming his son, directing him to the ram prepared to be offered instead of his son. God then blessed Abraham: "Because you have done this thing, and have not withheld your son, your only son—blessing I will bless you, and multiplying I will multiply your descendants as the stars of the heaven and as the sand which is on the seashore." This is a candid indication of his children through faith and baptism (symbolic of slaying his son). Isaac's sacrifice was symbolic of the Savior's death: he was slain by intention and returned alive, and Christ the Master died and rose. Likewise, as baptism is symbolic of the mystery of Christ's death and resurrection, Isaac's slaughter is symbolic of baptism in which the child is buried and snatched, purified from sin (vv. 16–17).

Second Prophecy Isaiah 45:11–17

His salvation for them: In this prophecy, Almighty God speaks of: His omnipotence that created the heavens and earth and those who dwell in them; His special people Israel: "I have raised him up in righteousness, and I will direct all his ways"; the disgrace of the makers of idols; and Israel's salvation: "But Israel shall be saved by the Lord with an everlasting salvation." This prophecy, specific to salvation (salvation based on baptism), completes the previous prophecy concerning baptism (vv. 13, 17).

Third Prophecy Proverbs 9:12–18

Warning them against sin: In this prophecy, Wisdom commands the baptized to avoid the paths of sin—here symbolized by the foolish, clamorous, ignorant woman who sits at the door of her house to entice the passerby saying: "'Stolen water is sweet, and bread eaten in secret is pleasant.' But he does not know that the dead are there, that her guests are in the depths of hell" (vv. 17–18).

Fourth Prophecy Job 36:1–33

Urging them to magnify His works: Here, Elihu points out to Job that God is just in all His ways, and that Job's sins keep goodness and blessings from him, then he commands him: "Remember to magnify His work, of which men have sung," enumerating for him some of these mighty works by which the Almighty is exalted (v. 24).

Fifth Prophecy Job 37:1–24

Fearing Him: This prophecy continues the meaning of the previous one as Elihu continues with another list of God's works: "Listen to this, O Job; stand still and consider the wondrous works of God," then stresses to Job: "As for the Almighty, we cannot find Him; He is excellent in power, in judgment and abundant justice; He does not oppress," finally commanding him: "Therefore men fear Him; He shows no partiality to any who are wise of heart" (vv. 14, 23, 24).

Sixth Prophecy Tobit[38]

Saving them: The book of Tobit fulfills the meaning of the previous prophecy, applying the psalm that says, "The angel of the Lord encamps all around those who fear Him, and delivers them" (Ps 34:7). The intention of reading it here is, first, to confirm God's use of His angels to rescue those who fear Him, and second, to reveal the book's solid connection with the issue of baptism. Rescuing Tobias from death is akin to saving Isaac from being sacrificed—both symbolic of baptism. The church has divided this book into 6 parts that symbolically point to the following spiritual aspects of baptism:

1. Tobit = The godfather/godmother
2. Sarah = The baptism (the door to membership in the church)
3. Archangel Raphael = The priest officiating this sacrament
4. Tobias = The baptized child
5. Tobit recovers his vision = Joy over the baptized's membership in the church
6. Death of sin = Thanking God for deliverance from death (death of sin)

Part One (Tobit 1:1–3:6)

Tobit's test: Tobit was a righteous man from the tribe of Naphtali whose city is above Galilee. He would travel to Jerusalem to worship the Lord in His temple and distribute the tithes to the needy and strangers. His wife Anna bore him one son whom he named Tobias

[38] All references in Tobit are taken from the DRA (Douay-Rheims American Edition), as it is most compatible with the Arabic, except for the last reference as noted.

and taught from childhood the fear of God. When he, his wife, his son, and his tribe were captured and taken to the city of Nineveh, he continued to remember the Lord with all his heart, so He gave him favor before King Shalmaneser. Finding his kinsman Gabael in need, he lent him 10 pieces of silver (remaining from what the king had granted him) and took a promissory note. He diligently continued feeding the hungry, clothing the naked, and burying the dead and those killed by King Sennacherib (Shalmaneser's successor). One day, exhausted from burying the bodies of the children of Israel whom the king killed in his hatred, he came to his house and slept alongside a wall, "And as he was sleeping, hot dung out of a swallow's nest fell upon his eyes, and he was made blind. Now this trial the Lord therefore permitted to happen to him, that an example might be given to posterity of his patience, as also of holy Job." Despite all this he was not disgruntled, although his friends reproached him severely (even his wife reproached him) to the point that his soul loathed life and he asked God to relieve him from it (2:11–12).

No doubt, Tobit's test greatly resembles Abraham's, where he was asked to offer his son a sacrifice, and Job's, where he lost all his wealth, children, and health, to be an example of patience to all in times of temptation.

Part Two (Tobit 3:7–23)

Sarah's sadness and hope: Now, in Rages, Sarah, the only daughter of Raguel, was reproached by one of her father's maids because she had married seven husbands, and a demon killed each of them as they came to her. Sarah was grieved over this reproach and fasted three days praying to God in tears to remove her reproach: "Thou knowest, O Lord, that I never coveted a husband, and have kept my soul clean from all lust... But a husband I consented to take, with Thy fear, not with my lust," concluding her prayer: "For Thou art not delighted in our being lost, because after a storm Thou makest a calm, and after tears and weeping Thou pourest in joyfulness" (3:16–18, 22).

This Sarah, the only daughter to her father, who is adorned with purity and chastity, who awaits her bridegroom in the fear of God is symbolic of the one church of Christ who opens her bosom for the righteous children to enter into her, becoming her members through the one baptism so that she rejoices in them; her sadness over the death of sin (which infests people who do not believe in Christ the Master because of Satan's control over them) dissolves. The baptismal font continually awaits the approach of the estranged.

Part Three (Tobit 3:24–6:9)

Archangel Raphael's help: Sarah and Tobit's prayers were simultaneously heard, and God sent Archangel Raphael to rescue them. When Tobit felt that his prayer "that he might die" was heard, he called his only son Tobias and gave him many commandments, and commanded him to find a trustworthy travel companion to go reclaim his trust that was kept with Gabelus. Divine Economy provided him with a young fellow ready for travel who is later revealed as Archangel Raphael. The young man went with Tobias to see his father, to comfort him that they would return safely, and that his eyesight would return on the condition that he would have a courageous heart. After Tobias took leave of his father and mother (who cried severely over losing her son), he left with the young man to fulfill his assignment (4:1).

As they spent the night next to the River Tigris, and when Tobias went down to wash his feet, a great fish leapt on him wanting to swallow him, so he called out to his companion, who directed him to drag it onto shore, which he did. Next, he directed him to, "take out the entrails of this fish, and lay up his heart, and his gall, and his liver for thee: for these are necessary for useful medicines." When Tobias asked for clarification, he informed him that if part of the heart and liver were placed over coals, its smoke would drive away demons from people not to return, and if the gall anoints blinded eyes, their vision returns (6:5).

Divine Economy reveals that the angel represents the priest who officiates the baptismal sacrament for the baptized. As the angel promised Tobit the return of his son and of his eyesight if he can "be of good courage," likewise the godfather rejoices through his courageous faith in salvation that saves his baptized child. In the next part of this story, the role of the priest is further enhanced (5:13).

Part Four (Tobit 6:10–9:12)

Rescuing Tobias: When Tobias wished to lodge, the angel guided him to the house of his kinsman, Raguel, who had an only daughter named Sarah, and then he took to enticing him to marry her for her father's wealth and her decency of character. When Tobias objected that her seven husbands were killed by a demon, the angel answered: "Hear me, and I will shew thee who they are, over whom the devil can prevail. For they who in such manner receive matrimony, as to shut out God from themselves, and from their mind, and to give themselves to their lust." He gave him certain commandments to follow with her to be rescued from the demon, and Tobias rejoiced (6:17–18).

They journeyed to the house of Raguel, and after a short conversation it became apparent that he was Tobias' uncle. After they prepared the food, Tobias declared his wish to marry Sarah, and Raguel hesitated because of the experiences with the seven previous husbands, yet the angel comforted him that this is according to God's will, so he consented immediately and handed Sarah to Tobias.

After dinner, Tobias retreated with Sarah and followed the angel's commands. He took the heart and liver out of his bag and cast them on the coals. When the demon smelled them, he fled to the wilderness of Egypt where the angel bound him. Then he said to her, "Sarah, arise, and let us pray to God today, and tomorrow, and the next day: because for these three nights we are joined to God: and when the third night is over, we will be in our own wedlock. For we are the children of saints." While they did this, Raguel had prepared a grave in which to bury Tobias, believing that he will also die like the seven other husbands, but when morning came and he found him alive, he and his wife blessed God and prepared a wedding feast for 14 days, giving him half their wealth to return to his father in safety. Then, Tobias asked the angel to go collect the debt from Gabelus and bring him to the wedding, which they celebrated in the fear of God (8:4–5).

This part firmly represents the sacrament of baptism: as the angel guided Tobias to lodge in his uncle's house to marry Sarah, one from his own kinsfolk and not a foreigner, as his father commanded him, likewise the priest calls the baptized to baptism in order to become a member of the church of Christ. As the angel directed him to place the heart and liver on the fire for the demon to flee when he smells the smoke, likewise the baptized undergoes the rite of Renouncing Satan before baptism. As Tobias asked Sarah to pray for three nights "because for these three nights we are joined to God," likewise after Renouncing Satan, the baptized confesses Christ and the priest submerges him in the baptismal font three times in the name of the holy Trinity—by which he becomes a member of the church of Christ. As Tobias emerged alive after his first night in marriage to Sarah, likewise the baptized is reborn a second spiritual birth from the water and Spirit. As the angel instructed Tobias before going to his uncle's house: "And when the third night is past, thou shalt take the virgin with the fear of the Lord, moved rather for love of children than for lust, that in the seed of Abraham," likewise, after baptism the baptized produces the fruit of the Spirit as children of God (6:22).

Part Five (Tobit 10–11)

Tobit recovers his vision: Tobit and Anna were grieved because their son did not return on the appointed day, and Anna did not eat by day, but went along the way awaiting his return and spent the night mourning his fate. Raguel had wanted Tobias to remain with him, but he asked to return to his parents, so Raguel consented, giving him half his possessions of money and servants, blessed them, and sent them off with great comfort and commands. The angel suggested to Tobias that they go ahead of the rest in order to comfort Tobit. They went and Tobias took the gall with him. From afar, Anna caught sight of them, so she quickly went to tell her husband. At this point, the angel advised Tobias to anoint the eyes of his father with the gall for his eyesight to return. Tobias rushed to greet his father, and they worshipped God thankfully. Then Tobias anointed Tobit's eyes "and a white skin began to come out of his eyes, like the skin of an egg. And Tobias took hold of it, and drew it from his eyes, and recovered his sight." After some days, Tobias' wife arrived with the rest of the company, and Tobit went out to greet her and blessed her, and all rejoiced greatly for seven days (11:14–15).

Tobit's regained sight, his joy over his son's rescue, and Tobias' return with his wife all represent the communal joy over the membership of the baptized in the church of Christ.

Part Six (Tobit 12–14)

Mercy delivers: Tobit advised his son to pay the wages of the angel, so Tobias recounted all the good the man had done to them and suggested giving him half of everything they returned with. Tobit agreed and they called the man and made this offer. The man took them aside and commanded them to bless God and reveal His works and continue praying and almsgiving. Then, he revealed to them that he is the one who offered up their prayers before the Lord, being Raphael one of the seven who stand before God to present to Him the prayers of the saints. When they heard this, they were shocked, but he calmed them and commanded them to write down their story. Then, he disappeared from their sight, so Tobit offered up a long thanksgiving prayer to God for his great works. Tobit continued to be charitable until his old age, and called his son and six grandsons, commanding them to leave Nineveh and continue performing deeds of mercy: "So now, my children, consider what almsgiving accomplishes and how righteousness delivers [from the snares of death prepared for him]... But before he died he heard of the destruction of Nineveh, which Nebuchadnezzar and Ahasuerus had captured. Before his death he rejoiced over Nineveh" (RSV 14:11, 15).

This part of the book of Tobit wants to reveal to the children of baptism that mercy delivers from death, and the penalty of sin is death, as in the case of Nineveh.

PSALMS AND GOSPELS

Matins Psalm — Psalms 51:7–8

Speaking for those who believe in Christ and come forward to receive the sacrament of baptism, this psalm asks God to purge them of sin, so that they would rejoice in being considered children of light (as mentioned in the accompanying gospel passage): "Purge me with hyssop, and I shall be clean; wash me, and I shall be whiter than snow. Make me hear joy and gladness, that the bones You have broken may rejoice."

Matins Gospel John 3:14–21

This passage speaks of the Savior justifying those who receive the sacrament of baptism, as He told Nicodemus: "He who believes in Him is not condemned; but he who does not believe is condemned already, because he has not believed in the name of the only begotten Son of God" (v. 18).

Liturgy Psalm Psalms 34:5, 4

The first half of this psalm encourages those who accept the faith to receive the sacrament of baptism and become radiant. The second half refers to the accompanying gospel passage, in which Nicodemus sought Christ the Master in the middle of the night to help him understand what is difficult for him, and the Savior's response to his request: "They looked to Him and were radiant, and their faces were not ashamed. I sought the Lord, and He heard me."

Liturgy Gospel John 3:1–13

In this passage, the Savior urges the new birth in baptism, which is necessary to win the kingdom, as He told Nicodemus: "Most assuredly, I say to you, unless one is born of water and the Spirit, he cannot enter the kingdom of God" (v. 5).

EPISTLES

The Pauline Epistle 1 Corinthians 10:1–13

Warning the baptized against relapsing into sin after baptism: Beginning by showing that many of the Old Testament events were symbolic of the New Testament sacraments, the apostle says concerning baptism: "All were baptized into Moses in the cloud and in the sea." Concerning Christ the Master's body and blood he says, "All ate the same spiritual food, and all drank the same spiritual drink. For they drank of that spiritual Rock that followed them, and that Rock was Christ," proceeding to show that their punishment was a warning to us: "Now all these things happened to them as examples, and they were written for our admonition, upon whom the ends of the ages have come." He then commands: "Therefore let him who thinks he stands take heed lest he fall," it is the duty of the baptized who were purified of sin to be watchful against falling into it once more, so as not to receive the same fate as the children of Israel (vv. 2, 3–4, 11, 12).

The Catholic Epistle 1 John 2:12–17

Do not love the world: Here, John writes to the fathers, young men, and little children, commending their way and commanding all not to love the world because all that is in it is: "The lust of the flesh, the lust of the eyes, and the pride of life" —matters that are not from the Father, but from the world. He says, "Do not love the world or the things in the world" (vv. 16, 15).

The Acts Acts 8:9–17

Receiving the Holy Spirit after baptism: This passage shows that when the people of Samaria believed and were baptized at the hands of Philip the deacon, even Simon the magician joined them, being astonished when he saw the signs and wonders. When the apostles in Jerusalem heard of the faith of Samaria, they sent John and Peter to them, who laid their hands on them, and they received the Holy Spirit after being baptized in the name of the Lord Jesus.

SIXTH WEEK – SATURDAY
SALVATION OF BAPTISM

Linking the Readings:

All the readings of this day center on one theme: **Salvation of baptism**—salvation to those who believe in the Lord and are baptized, as the Gospel states: "He who believes and is baptized will be saved" (Mark 16:16)

In the Matins Gospel, the **Savior forgives believers' sins**, as He forgave the sins of the paralytic let down from the ceiling when He saw the faith of those who brought him; while the Liturgy Gospel speaks of **His salvation for them**, as He told blind Bartimaeus, "Your faith has saved you."

The Pauline Epistle speaks of the **grace poured out by Christ the Master on the baptized**, as the apostle told the believers that to each one of them grace was given according to the measure of Christ's gift; in the Catholic Epistle, Peter **exhorts them to holiness**, as he says, "You also be holy in all your conduct"; and the Acts reading speaks of **Him delivering them from danger**, as Paul and his companions were saved from the dangers at sea.

PSALMS AND GOSPELS

Matins Psalm — Psalms 79:8–9

Speaking for sinners who are symbolized by the paralytic let down from the ceiling (mentioned in the accompanying gospel passage), and whose spiritual condition has been brought very low because of the multitude of their sins, this psalm asks God to remember them in His tender mercy: "Let Your tender mercies come speedily to meet us, for we have been brought very low. Help us, O God of our salvation, for the glory of Your name."

Matins Gospel Matthew 9:1–8

In this passage, the Savior forgives the sins of believers, as He told the paralytic after seeing the faith of those who brought him, "Your sins are forgiven you" (v. 2).

Liturgy Psalm Psalms 32:1–2

This psalm blesses believers whose transgression God forgave, not imputing their iniquity, not attributing their sin to them: "Blessed is he whose transgression is forgiven, whose sin is covered. Blessed is the man to whom the Lord does not impute iniquity."

Liturgy Gospel Mark 10:46–52

This passage shows that the Lord Jesus renders His salvation to believers baptized into Him, as He told blind Bartimaeus, "Your faith has saved you,"[39] as opening the eyes of the blind is symbolic of enlightening the vision through baptism (v. 52).

EPISTLES

The Pauline Epistle Ephesians 4:1–7

Grace poured out on the baptized by Christ the Master: In this passage, the apostle commands believers to preserve the unity of the Spirit, because they are one body, having, "One Lord, one faith, one

[39] The New Jerusalem Bible (NJB) was used for compatibility with the Arabic.

baptism," revealing to them the grace they received and its value: "But to each one of us grace was given according to the measure of Christ's gift" (vv. 5, 7).

The Catholic Epistle 1 Peter 1:13–21

Exhorting them to holiness: Here, Peter encourages them to holiness: "As He who called you is holy, you also be holy in all your conduct," reminding them of the value of their grand redemption, which demands this holiness: "You were not redeemed with corruptible things... but with the precious blood of Christ, as of a lamb without blemish and without spot" (vv. 15, 18–19).

The Acts Acts 27:9–26

Delivering them from danger: This passage completes the previous meaning, showing that God delivers believers who have received the grace of baptism and live in holiness. It recounts the story of Paul and his companions traveling by sea to Rome, and his prophecy of the upcoming dangers at sea and how his travel companions did not believe him. After the storm rose against them and all hope of being saved was lost, Paul said: "Men, you should have listened to me... And now I urge you to take heart, for there will be no loss of life among you, but only of the ship." This is because an angel had said to him, "God has granted you all those who sail with you" (vv. 21–22, 24).

SIXTH WEEK – SUNDAY
ENLIGHTENMENT OF BAPTISM[40]

Linking the Readings:

All the readings of this day center on one theme: **The enlightenment of baptism**—illuminating the vision of those who receive the sacrament of baptism

In the Vespers Gospel, the Savior urges them to **enter through the narrow gate (bearing the difficulties of the holy life)**, as He commanded the man who asked Him, "Lord, are there few who are saved?" In the Matins Gospel, **He warns against hypocrisy**, as He warned His disciples and the multitudes against imitating the hypocrisy of the scribes and Pharisees. In the Liturgy Gospel, the Savior **promises to restore their vision**, symbolized in giving sight to the man born blind. And in the Evening Gospel, He has **compassion on them**, as He had compassion on the blind man of Bethsaida and restored his vision.

In the Pauline Epistle, Paul charges them to **be spiritually renewed after being baptized**, as he commanded to put off the old man and put on the new man; in the Catholic Epistle, John promises them **God's response to their prayers** offered up for themselves and for others; and the Acts reading speaks of **God consoling them in hardships**, as Paul affirmed to his companions in the tempest tossed ship that not a hair of their heads would fall.

---

[40] This Sunday is known as Baptism Sunday, as on this day it is a church custom to present catechumens and infants to receive the sacrament of baptism. Their souls would then cry out with the man born blind, "I was blind but now I see."

PSALMS AND GOSPELS

Vespers Psalm — Psalms 17:3, 5

Speaking for the baptized who vowed through their baptism to walk uprightly (these are the ones who the Savior urges in the accompanying gospel passage to enter through the narrow gate), this psalm confesses God's trials befalling them to test their purity (the narrow gate), then petitions Him to confirm them in His truth: "You have tested my heart; You have visited me in the night; You have tried me [by fire] and have found nothing. Uphold my steps in Your paths, that my footsteps may not slip."

Vespers Gospel — Luke 13:22–35

In this passage, the Savior urges the baptized to enter through the narrow gate, enduring the hardships of the holy life in order to be saved, as He answered the one who asked Him if few would be saved: "Strive to enter through the narrow gate" (v. 24).

Matins Psalm — Psalms 26:2–3

Speaking for the baptized who have walked uprightly (without hypocrisy), this psalm asks God to test the purity of their hearts. In this is a reference to their fulfilling the Lord's commandments that the hypocritical Pharisees and scribes called others to fulfill but did not do themselves, as mentioned in the accompanying gospel passage. Then, the psalm asks God to protect their pure hearts and confesses the Lord's mercy that rescued them from the fate of the scribes and Pharisees, and Jerusalem, as mentioned in the end of the Gospel passage, and says, "Examine me, O Lord, and prove me; try my mind and my heart. For Your lovingkindness is before my eyes, and I have walked in Your truth."

Matins Gospel Matthew 23:1–39

In this passage, the Savior warns the baptized of hypocrisy, as He said of the scribes and Pharisees: "Whatever they tell you to observe, that observe and do, but do not do according to their works; for they say, and do not do" (v. 3).

Liturgy Psalm Psalm 143:7

Speaking for the man born blind mentioned in the accompanying gospel passage and who is symbolic of the unbeliever who does not yet come forward to baptism and who says that his spirit fails, this psalm asks God not to hide His face from him (to enlighten his vision by baptism), and to answer his prayer: "Answer me speedily, O Lord; my spirit fails! Do not hide Your face from me. Hear my prayer, O Lord, give ear to my supplications! In Your faithfulness."

Liturgy Gospel John 9:1–41

In this passage, the Savior enlightens the vision of the baptized, as He told the man born blind who believed in Him after He opened his eyes: "For judgment I have come into this world, that those who do not see may see, and that those who see may be made blind" (v. 39).

Evening Psalm Psalm 41:1

This psalm asks the baptized to be merciful to the poor and needy for the reward of this mercy is that they will be rescued from hardships (symbolic of the Savior's compassion on the blind man whose eyes He opened in the accompanying gospel passage), and therefore says:

"Blessed is he who considers the poor; the Lord will deliver him in time of trouble."

Evening Gospel Mark 8:22–26

In this passage, the Savior has compassion on the baptized and enlightens their vision, as He was compassionate on the blind man of Bethsaida and placed His hands on his eyes: "And he was restored and saw everyone clearly" (v. 25).

EPISTLES

The Pauline Epistle Colossians 3:5–17

Spiritually renewing the baptized: In this passage, the apostle charges the baptized to put to death their earthly members, as they put off the old man with his works and put on the new man who renews knowledge: "Therefore, as the elect of God, holy and beloved, put on tender mercies, kindness, humility... But above all these things put on love... And whatever you do in word or deed, do all in the name of the Lord Jesus, giving thanks to God the Father through Him" (vv. 12–17).

The Catholic Epistle 1 John 5:13–21

God answering their prayers: Here, the Apostle shows that according to the confidence we have in God, "If we ask anything according to His will, He hears us." And that our prayers for ourselves and for others are answered: "If anyone sees his brother sinning a sin which does not lead to death, he will ask, and He will give him life for those who commit sin not leading to death" (vv. 14, 16).

The Acts Acts 27:27–37

Consoling them in hardships: This passage describes the danger at sea that Paul and his companions endured when they encountered a fourteen day sea storm, in which they fasted, after which Paul urged them to eat, saying, "For this is for your survival, since not a hair will fall from the head of any of you." These words consoled and comforted them and they ate (v. 32).

WEEK 6: ANOINTING OF THE STRUGGLE (BAPTISM)

DAY	*PROPHECIES*		PSALMS & GOSPELS Matins	 Liturgy	*EPISTLES* *Pauline*	 *Catholicon*	 *Acts*
MONDAY: REPENTANCE OF BAPTISM	*1* ***Prov****: God calls sinners to repentance*	*2* ***Is****: He promises to forgive them*	He destroys the wicked negligent shepherds	He urge them to repent lest they perish	*Walking properly*	*Being humble and non-judgmental*	*Opponents' failed attempts*
	3 ***Job****: He gives them understanding*						
TUESDAY: CONFESSION OF BAPTISM	*1* ***Prov****: He urges faith-confession*	*2* ***Is****: God's comfort to confessors*	Believers who confess their faith are rejected	The Savior urges His disciples to confess their faith	*Urging believers to prophesy*	*Being doers of the word*	*Prevailing over magic*
	3 ***Job****: Delegates ransom them*			*4* ***2 Kin****: Free ransom*			
WEDNESDAY: JUDGMENT OF BAPTISM	*1* ***Ex****: God threatens to punish unjust shepherds*	*2* ***Is****: He redeems His faithful people*	He reprimands shepherds who are hypocrites	The Savior condemns hypocritical shepherds	*Judging hypocritical shepherds*	*Their destruction is strong*	*Being confronted*
	3 ***Prov****: He quickens them*			*4* ***Job****: Submitting to Him*		*5* ***Sirach****: Their honor*	
THURSDAY: LIFE OF BAPTISM	*1* ***2 King****: Shepherds restore believers*	*2* ***Is****: He supports shepherds for the believers*	The Savior destroys wicked shepherds	He gives believers life	*Urging believers to godliness*	*Concern for the salvation of others*	*Exposure to dangers*
	3 ***Prov****: Prolonging their lives*		*4* ***Job****: Answering their petitions*		*5* ***Sirach****: His commandments to them*		
FRIDAY: RESURRECTION OF BAPTISM	*1* ***Gen****: He resurrects the baptized*	*2* ***Is****: His salvation for them*	The Savior pardons the baptized	He urges them to baptism	*Warning the baptized from relapsing*	*Do not love the world*	*Receiving the Holy Spirit*
	3 ***Prov****: Warning against sins*		*4* ***Job****: Magnifying His works*		*5* ***Job****: Fearing Him*		*6* ***Tobit****: Saving them*
SATURDAY: SALVATION OF BAPTISM			He forgives believers' sins	His salvation for believers	*Christ's grace poured out on the baptized*	*Exhorting them to holiness*	*Delivering them from danger*
SUNDAY: ENLIGHTENMENT OF BAPTISM	**Vespers Gospel** Entering through the narrow gate	**Matins Gospel** He warns the baptized against hypocrisy	**Liturgy Gospel** He promises to restore their vision	**Evening Gospel** His compassion on them	*Spiritually renewing the baptized*	*God answering their prayers*	*Consoling them in hardships*

UNIVERSAL THEME:

VICTORY OF THE STRUGGLE (THE SAVIOR)

SEVENTH WEEK – MONDAY
THE SAVIOR'S WITNESSES

Linking the Readings:

All the readings of this day center on one theme: **The Savior's witnesses**—the evidences witnessing to Jesus as the Savior of the world, leading those who accept them to eternal life

In the first prophecy, the Sage mentions some **virtues leading those adorned with them to eternal life**, such as the wisdom and righteousness mentioned in Proverbs; the second prophecy speaks of **God redeeming them**, as Isaiah the prophet mentions that God redeemed His servant Jacob and sent him Christ the Master; and the third prophecy speaks of **Him revealing His might to them**, as He revealed it to Job.

The Matins Gospel speaks of **His mercy to them**, as Abraham revealed to the rich man that he is tormented while Lazarus is comforted; and the Liturgy Gospel speaks of **Him giving life to those who accept evidence attesting to Him—the Gospel**—as the Savior asked the Jews to search the Scriptures which witness to Him, in which they assume they have eternal life.

In the Pauline Epistle, Paul points believers to **avoid stumbling blocks to the faith (which lead to destruction)** as the apostles commanded; in the Catholic Epistle, James speaks of **believers being merciful to the brethren**, as he says that "judgment is without mercy to the one who has shown no mercy"; and the Acts reading speaks of **their missionary success**, as Paul put the Jews and the Hellenists to shame so that the churches were multiplied.

PROPHECIES

First Prophecy — Proverbs 10:1–16

Virtues leading to eternal life: In this passage, Wisdom catalogs a plethora of various behavioral virtues and their contrasts, with the virtues leading to eternal life if the believer keeps them, such as: wisdom, righteousness, integrity, diligence, love, etc., unlike their contrasts: "The labor of the righteous leads to life, the wages of the wicked to sin" (v. 16).

Second Prophecy — Isaiah 48:17–49:4

God redeeming them: Here, Isaiah shows that God has redeemed His servant Jacob by releasing His people with His exalted strength from Babylon, continuing that He sent them His Son, as the Savior spoke of Himself: "The Lord has called Me from the womb; from the matrix of My mother He has made mention of My name." Thereafter, when His people rejected Him, He said, "I have labored in vain, I have spent my strength for nothing and in vain" (vv. 1, 4).

Third Prophecy — Job 38:1–36

Revealing His might to them: In this passage, God challenges Job to answer His questions, proving his foolishness and ignorance by listing examples of His exalted works, as the Almighty said: "Do you know the ordinances of the heavens? Can you set their dominion over the earth? Can you lift up your voice to the clouds, that an abundance of water may cover you? Can you send out lightnings, that they may go, and say to you, 'Here we are!'?" (vv. 33–35).

PSALMS AND GOSPELS

Matins Psalm — Psalms 32:10–11

The start of this psalm points to the pains of sinners (symbolized by the rich man in the accompanying gospel passage) and then talks about God's mercy on believers who endure the trials of faith (represented by Lazarus, who was laid at the rich man's gate). The psalm charges believers to rejoice in the Lord's mercy, with Lazarus who was comforted: "Many sorrows shall be to the wicked; but he who trusts in the Lord, mercy shall surround him. Be glad in the Lord and rejoice, you righteous; and shout for joy, all you upright in heart!"

Matins Gospel — Luke 16:19–31

This passage speaks of the Savior's mercy on believers who endure the trials of life, as Abraham spoke of Lazarus to the rich man in torments: "Son, remember that in your lifetime you received your good things, and likewise Lazarus evil things; but now he is comforted and you are tormented" (v. 25).

Liturgy Psalm — Psalms 86:12–13

Speaking for believers who searched the scriptures (as the Savior mentioned in the accompanying gospel passage) and believed in Christ, winning eternal life (being saved from Sheol), the psalm confesses God and glorifies Him for His mercy: "I will praise You, O Lord my God, with all my heart, and I will glorify Your name forevermore. For great is Your mercy toward me, and You have delivered my soul from the depths of Sheol."

Liturgy Gospel John 5:31–47

This passage speaks of the Savior giving life to those who receive the Holy Bible's witness about the validity of believing in Him, as He told the Jews: "You search the Scriptures, for in them you think you have eternal life; and these are they which testify of Me" (v.39).

EPISTLES

The Pauline Epistle Romans 14:10–15:2

Avoiding stumbling blocks to the faith: In this passage, the apostle charges believers not to offend each other because of food: "If your brother is grieved because of your food, you are no longer walking in love. Do not destroy with your food the one for whom Christ died," continuing, "It is good neither to eat meat nor drink wine nor do anything by which your brother stumbles or is offended or is made weak. Do you have faith? Have it to yourself before God," and concluding, "Let each of us please his neighbor for his good, leading to edification" (vv. 14:15, 21–22; 15:2).

The Catholic Epistle James 2:5–13

Believers' mercy on the brethren: Here, James shows how it is not fitting for believers to show partiality to the rich and disdain the poor: "If you show partiality, you commit sin, and are convicted by the law as transgressors," then he charges them to have mercy on such brethren: "For judgment is without mercy to the one who has shown no mercy. Mercy triumphs over judgment" (vv. 9, 13).

The Acts Acts 9:22–31

Their missionary success: This passage shows that at Saul's conversion to the faith, he took to preaching Christ, grew in strength, and put the Jews to shame, who in turn conspired (along with the Hellenists) to kill him, but he was saved from their hands. Based on this, the churches "had peace and were edified. And walking in the fear of the Lord and in the comfort of the Holy Spirit, they were multiplied" (v. 31).

SEVENTH WEEK – TUESDAY
CONFESSING THE SAVIOR

Linking the Readings:

All the readings of this day center on one theme: **Confessing the Savior**—confessing the Lord Jesus as the Savior of the world

The first prophecy speaks of the **steadfastness of those who confess the faith**, as Solomon the Sage mentions in his Proverbs; the second prophecy speaks of **God's promises to them**, as Isaiah said that they will not hunger or thirst; the third prophecy speaks of **Him revealing His might to them**, as He revealed it to Job; and the fourth prophecy speaks of **urging them to repent**, as Jesus the son of Sirach mentions.

The Matins Gospel exhorts them to **forgive sins**, as the Savior commanded during His conversation with His disciples; while the Liturgy Gospel speaks of Him **glorifying those who confess Him**, as the evangelist blamed the Jews who believed in the Savior for not confessing Him for fear of the Pharisees "for they loved the praise of men more than the praise of God."

In the Pauline Epistle, Paul **urges believers not to be content with speaking in tongues, but also to interpret**; in the Catholic Epistle, Peter **urges believers to walk in holiness**; and the Acts reading speaks of them **being exposed to suffering for His sake**, as Paul was examined under scourging to discover the reason the Jews complained against him.

PROPHECIES

First Prophecy — Proverbs 10:17–32

Steadfastness of those who confess the faith: In this passage, Wisdom lists another plethora of various behavioral virtues and their contrasts (besides the ones in the first prophecy on Monday), which point to the steadfastness of the righteous who confess the faith. In it, the Sage says: "The tongue of the righteous is choice silver... The lips of the righteous feed many... When the whirlwind passes by, the wicked is no more, but the righteous has an everlasting foundation... The righteous will never be removed, but the wicked will not inhabit the earth" (vv. 20, 21, 25, 30).

Second Prophecy — Isaiah 49:6–10

God's promises to them: Isaiah begins the chapter, from which this prophecy was taken, by mentioning how our Savior complains of the Jews to whom He was sent. In this prophecy, he shows that He will be sent (after the Jews) to the Gentiles who will accept Him, on whom He will pour out His rich promises: "They shall neither hunger nor thirst, neither heat nor sun shall strike them; for He who has mercy on them will lead them, even by the springs of water He will guide them" (v. 10).

Third Prophecy — Job 38:37–39:30

Revealing His might to them: In this prophecy, God illustrates His might to Job, as Job is ignorant and foolish concerning many issues, such as: creating rocks, the dwelling of the deer, setting the wild donkey free, the reliance of the wild ox, the ostrich's lack of understanding, the horse's raging into dangers, the hawk spreading its wings, and the eagle mounting up and dwelling in the rocks.

Fourth Prophecy Sirach 5:1–15[41]

Urging them to repent: In this prophecy, the son of Sirach urges believers not to delay repentance, "Do not delay to turn to the Lord, nor postpone it from day to day; for suddenly the wrath of the Lord will go forth, and at the time of punishment you will perish," concluding the commandments in a general sense: "In great and small matters do not act amiss" (RSV: Sir 5:7, 15).

PSALMS AND GOSPELS

Matins Psalm Psalms 38:18–19

Speaking for those confessing their iniquities, this psalm begins by mentioning their repentance and then ends with their exposure to the wrongs of others (mentioned in the accompanying gospel passage as the overpowering enemies whom they forgive): "For I will declare my iniquity; I will be in anguish over my sin. But my enemies are vigorous, and they are strong."

Matins Gospel Luke 17:1–10

In this passage, the Savior urges believers to forgive: "If your brother sins against you, rebuke him; and if he repents, forgive him" (v. 3).

Liturgy Psalm Psalms 51:2–3

Speaking for those confessing their iniquities, this psalm begs God to purify them as they confess these sins to Him: "Wash me

[41] This prophecy was removed in the new Katameros without justification, as it completes the meaning.

thoroughly from my iniquity, and cleanse me from my sin. For I acknowledge my transgressions, and my sin is always before me."

Liturgy Gospel John 12:36–43

This passage speaks of the Savior's glory to those who confess Him. The evangelist mentioned that many rulers believed in the Savior, "but because of the Pharisees they did not confess Him, lest they should be put out of the synagogue; for they loved the praise of men more than the praise of God," [as contrasted with Isaiah who was worthy to see His glory v.41] (vv. 42–43).

EPISTLES

The Pauline Epistle 1 Corinthians 14:5–17

Urging believers to prophesy: In this passage, the apostle urges believers to prophesy, because prophecy is greater than speaking with tongues, giving the example of a musical instrument: if the trumpet makes an uncertain sound, who will prepare for war? He charges them not to be satisfied with speaking in tongues, but to endeavor to interpret, "So likewise you, unless you utter by the tongue words easy to understand, how will it be known what is spoken? ... [He charges] Let him who speaks in a tongue pray that he may interpret" (vv. 9, 13).

The Catholic Epistle 2 Peter 3:8–15

Urging them to holiness: In this passage, Peter urges believers to struggle towards repentance before the Day of the Lord comes since God is patient with them. He describes the coming of this Day and the passing away of the elements, and charges them (as they expect His coming) to pursue holiness: "Therefore, beloved, looking forward to these things, be diligent to be found by Him in peace, without spot and blameless" (v. 14).

The Acts Acts 22:17–24

Suffering pain for His sake: Here, Paul's address reveals how he was called to the apostolic service. When he reached the junction about his commission to the Gentiles, the [Jewish] listeners raised their voices against him, caused a ruckus, and threw dirt into the air to the point that "the commander ordered him to be brought into the barracks, and said that he should be examined under scourging, so that he might know why they shouted so against him" (v. 24).

SEVENTH WEEK –WEDNESDAY
FAITH IN THE SAVIOR

Linking the Readings:

All the readings of this day center on one theme: **Faith in the Savior**—faith that inherits eternal life and resurrection for the believer on the Last Day

The first prophecy speaks of **God's salvation for believers**, as Proverbs mentions that "the righteousness of the upright will deliver them"; the second prophecy speaks of **His promises to them**, as He promised the righteous, on the tongue of Isaiah, that their light shall dawn in the darkness and He shall satisfy their soul in drought; and the third prophecy speaks of **revealing His might to them, with which He fulfills His promises to them**, as He revealed to Job in His answers to him out of the whirlwind.

In the Matins Gospel, He **urges the faithful to examine the hardships of discipleship to Him before beginning**, as He gave them the parables of the tower builder and the king who went out to make war against one who is stronger; while the Liturgy Gospel promises to **give life to those who believe in Him**, as He attested that "everyone who sees the Son and believes in Him may have everlasting life."

In the Pauline Epistle, Paul speaks of **the salvation of those coming to the faith**, as he attested to those who confess with their mouths and believe; in the Catholic Epistle, James commends believers to a **faith with meekness**, to accept the word implanted in them with meekness; and the Acts reading speaks of the **uproar against them because of their faith**, as Demetrius the silversmith incited the crowd against Paul.

PROPHECIES

First Prophecy Proverbs 10:32–11:13

God's salvation for believers: This prophecy includes a plethora of various behavioral virtues and their contrasts which reveal that righteousness rescues from death, as the Sage speaks: "The righteousness of the upright will deliver them, but the unfaithful will be caught by their lust... The righteous is delivered from trouble, and it comes to the wicked instead" (vv. 11:6, 8).

Second Prophecy Isaiah 58:1–11

His promises to them: In this prophecy, Isaiah rebukes the hypocrisy of those pretending godliness, giving the example of their fake fasts when compared to the genuine fast. Then, God pours out His promises to those who are righteous: "If you take away the yoke from your midst... If you extend your soul to the hungry and satisfy the afflicted soul, then your light shall dawn in the darkness, and your darkness shall be as the noonday... And satisfy your soul in drought" (vv. 9–11).

Third Prophecy Job 40:1–41:34

Revealing His might to them: In this passage, when Job [finally] humbled himself before the Lord, Almighty God deliberately provoked Job, to drive him to confess God's righteousness, might, and wisdom. First, He spoke to him of the behemoth that He created, showing that he eats grass like oxen. Then He spoke to him of Leviathan and the great power the Almighty gave him: "Strength dwells in his neck... When he raises himself up, the mighty are afraid... He regards iron as straw, and bronze as rotten wood... On earth there is nothing like him, which is made without fear" (vv. 41:22, 25, 27, 33).

PSALMS AND GOSPELS

Matins Psalm — Psalm 57:1

Speaking for the faithful who rely on God's help to overcome hardships that pursue the Lord Jesus' followers—hating family and carrying the cross, the difficulties they must think about before deciding to follow Him (as mentioned in the accompanying gospel passage)—this psalm asks God to have mercy on them and help them until these calamities have passed by, until they overcome these hardships: "Be merciful to me, O God, be merciful to me! For my soul trusts in You; and in the shadow of Your wings I will make my refuge, until these calamities have passed by."

Matins Gospel — Luke 14:28–35

In this passage, the Savior urges the faithful to consider the hardships they will face, before deciding to follow Him, as He illustrates by telling the parable of building the tower and the king who went out to make war against one stronger than him, concluding: "So likewise, whoever of you does not forsake all that he has cannot be My disciple" (v. 33).

Liturgy Psalm — Psalms 51:2–3

Speaking for the faithful who confess their iniquities, for the Father to draw them to come to the Lord Jesus (as mentioned in the accompanying gospel passage), this psalm asks God to cast away their iniquities: "Wash me thoroughly from my iniquity, and cleanse me from my sin. For I acknowledge my transgressions, and my sin is always before me."

Liturgy Gospel John 6:35–45

This passage speaks of the Savior giving life to those who believe in Him, as He said, "Everyone who sees the Son and believes in Him may have everlasting life; and I will raise him up at the last day" (v. 40).

EPISTLES

The Pauline Epistle Romans 10:4–13

Salvation of those coming to the faith: In this passage, the apostle makes a distinction between the righteousness of the law and the righteousness that is by faith: "If you confess with your mouth the Lord Jesus and believe in your heart that God has raised Him from the dead, you will be saved," concluding, "Whoever calls on the name of the Lord shall be saved" (vv. 9, 13).

The Catholic Epistle James 1:13–21

Faith with meekness: Beginning in this passage, James commands the faithful not to assume that the temptations they face are coming from God because the Almighty cannot be tempted by evil, nor does He tempt anyone, but actually, "Each one is tempted when he is drawn away by his own desires and enticed." Then he commands all to "lay aside all filthiness and overflow of wickedness, and receive with meekness the implanted word, which is able to save your souls" (vv. 14, 21).

The Acts Acts 19:23–26

Uproar against them: This passage shows that "about that time there arose a great commotion about the Way," at which point

Demetrius the silversmith incited the craftsmen of silver shrines for Diana against Paul, because Paul had cried out saying, "They are not gods which are made with hands" (vv. 23, 26).

SEVENTH WEEK – THURSDAY
RESURRECTION OF THE SAVIOR

Linking the Readings:

All the readings of this day center on one theme: **Resurrection of the Savior**—Him raising believers on the last day

The first prophecy speaks of **God giving life to the faithful**, as Proverbs declared that righteousness leads to life and evil leads to death; the second prophecy speaks of **His blessings to them**, as God said on the tongue of Isaiah that His servants will drink, but those who abandoned Him will thirst; the third prophecy speaks of **them submitting to Him**, as Job submitted to Him and said, "Therefore, I abhor myself, and repent in dust and ashes"; and the fourth prophecy speaks of **destroying those who do not believe in the resurrection**, as the officer in Samaria who did not believe Elisha perished.

The Matins Gospel speaks of the Savior **glorifying humble believers**, as He told His disciples who grumbled against the petition of the mother of Zebedee's sons that "whoever desires to become great among you, let him be your servant"; while the Liturgy Gospel speaks of **Him resurrecting them on Judgment Day**, as He revealed to the Sadducees that He is the God of the living, not the dead.

The Pauline Epistle speaks of **the believers' awaited resurrection**, as the apostle said that "He who raised up the Lord Jesus will also raise us up"; in the Catholic Epistle, John exhorts them in the need to **love one another**; and the Acts reading speaks of them **enduring opposition for accepting the doctrine of Resurrection**, as Paul was brought to court for this reason.

PROPHECIES

First Prophecy — Proverbs 11:13–26

Giving life to the faithful: This prophecy includes a plethora of various behavioral virtues and their contrasts, rewarding the first and punishing the second, as the Sage says, "As righteousness leads to life, so he who pursues evil pursues it to his own death" (v. 19).

Second Prophecy — Isaiah 65:8–16

His blessings to His servants: In this prophecy, God says that He "will bring forth descendants from Jacob, and from Judah an heir of My mountain; and My elect shall inherit it." Then, He shows that He will number those who left Him for the sword, and finally, addresses them (revealing His blessings to His servants): "Behold, My servants shall eat, but you shall be hungry; behold, My servants shall drink, but you shall be thirsty; behold, My servants shall rejoice, but you shall be ashamed" (v. 9, 13).

Third Prophecy — Job 42:1–6

Submitting to Him: In this passage, after Job listened to the Almighty Lord's speech about His mighty power, he responded in submission to Him: "I have heard of You by the hearing of the ear, but now my eye sees You. Therefore I abhor myself, and repent in dust and ashes" (vv. 5–6).

Fourth Prophecy 2 Kings 6:8–7:20[42]

Destroying unbelievers: This prophecy tells of the king of Syria and his armies encamping against Samaria causing a dreadful famine to the point that women ate their children. Then, it tells that Elisha gave the hopeful prophecy of abundance in Samaria but the king's officer refused to believe, so Elisha responded: "In fact, you shall see it with your eyes, but you shall not eat of it." The passage continues to prove the actuality of the prophecy and the death of the unbelieving officer who was trampled by the people (v. 2).

PSALMS AND GOSPELS

Matins Psalm Psalm 63:1

The start of this psalm points to the accompanying gospel passage in which the mother of Zebedee's sons went to the Savior with a petition, and then speaking for believers who want the Savior to raise them with Him on the last day, this psalm confesses that the way to greatness among believers in this world is humility, which is called a flesh longing in a dry and thirsty land. Thus, the psalm says: "O God, You are my God; early will I seek You; my soul thirsts for You; my flesh longs for You in a dry and thirsty land where there is no water."

Matins Gospel Matthew 20:20–28

In this passage, the Savior glorifies the humble believers, as He told His disciples who grumbled against Zebedee's sons' petition: "Yet it

---

[42] This prophecy was removed in the new Katameros without justification, as it completes the meaning.

shall not be so among you; but whoever desires to become great among you, let him be your servant" (v. 26).

Liturgy Psalm Psalms 122:1–2

Speaking for believers whom the Savior raises on the last day, who will be like angels in heaven when they rise from the dead as mentioned in the accompanying gospel passage, the psalm rejoices in going to heaven and standing in heavenly Jerusalem: "I was glad when they said to me, let us go into the house of the Lord. Our feet have been standing within your gates, O Jerusalem!"

Liturgy Gospel Mark 12:18–27

This passage speaks of the Savior raising believers on judgment day, as He told the Sadducees who asked Him of the fate of the woman who had seven husbands: "But concerning the dead, that they rise, have you not read in the book of Moses, in the burning bush passage, how God spoke to him, saying, 'I am the God of Abraham, the God of Isaac, and the God of Jacob'? He is not the God of the dead, but the God of the living." (vv. 26–27).

EPISTLES

The Pauline Epistle 2 Corinthians 4:5–18

The believers' awaited resurrection: In this passage, the apostle reveals that the hardships and afflictions that he endured during his evangelic ministry led to: first, glorifying God's might; second, to benefiting the faithful; and third: to their resurrection on the last day, as he said openly, "And since we have the same spirit of faith, according to what is written, "I believed and therefore I spoke," we also believe and therefore speak, knowing that He who raised up the Lord Jesus will also raise us up with Jesus, and will present us with you" (vv. 13–14).

The Catholic Epistle 1 John 3:13–24

Loving one another: In this passage, John mentions that the faithful have been transferred from death to life by loving the brethren and then commands that love must be in deed and truth, not by words and in tongue. Once they fulfill this, whatever they ask of Him they will receive, because they kept His commandments, and clarifies this by saying: "And this is His commandment: that we should believe on the name of His Son Jesus Christ and love one another, as He gave us commandment" (v. 23).

The Acts Acts 25:23–26:6

Enduring opposition because of the Resurrection: When the Jews presented their complaints against Paul because of his belief in the resurrection from the dead, he was brought to judgment before King Agrippa. When the king permitted him to defend himself, he began giving a synopsis of his life since his youth, confirming his commitment to his ancestral doctrine as a Pharisee and said, "According to the strictest sect of our religion I lived a Pharisee. And now I stand and am judged for the hope of the promise made by God to our fathers" (vv. 5–6).

SEVENTH WEEK – FRIDAY
THE SAVIOR'S JUDGMENT[43]

Linking the Readings:

All the readings of this day center on one theme: **The Savior's judgment**—His just judgment on judgment day to all people for their endeavors in this life

The first prophecy speaks of **the favorable end to the believers' strife**, as Jacob-Israel's life came to a favorable end, as well as that of his son Joseph. The second prophecy speaks of **God's reward to them**, as the Sage revealed in Proverbs the reward to the righteous and the punishment of the wicked. The third prophecy speaks of Him **perpetuating their name and posterity**, as the Lord declared on the tongue of Isaiah that He will perpetuate the name and posterity of all who believe in Him from all nations. The fourth prophecy speaks of **Him blessing their end**, as He blessed the later days of Job, after his temptation had ended.

The Matins Gospel speaks of the Savior **choosing those who are prepared at His second coming**, as the Lord of Glory mentioned in His conversation with His disciples; while the Liturgy Gospel speaks of **judging those who refuse the salvation offered to them**, as He prophesied of the destruction of Jerusalem who rejected the Savior.

In the Pauline Epistle, Paul **urges them to fulfill the spiritual ministry**, as he urged his disciple Timothy; in the Catholic Epistle, James exhorts them in **enduring hardships until they produce fruit**; and the Acts reading incites them to **visit the Gentiles also**, as Peter declared during his address on the issue of circumcision.

[43] This day is known as *Great Fast Concluding Friday* because it ends the Holy Forty Days Fast.

PROPHECIES

First Prophecy — Genesis 49:33–50:26

The favorable end to believers' striving: This passage begins with the death of Jacob, his son Joseph mourning over him, and the ensuing burial. Next, Joseph comforts his brothers who asked forgiveness, and at the age of 110 (after he saw his descendants to the third generation), he died, was embalmed, and was put in a coffin.

Second Prophecy — Proverbs 11:27–12:22

God rewards them: This prophecy includes a plethora of various behavioral virtues and their contrasts (all centering on the righteous finding favor and the wicked finding trouble), specifically, they show that the righteous "flourish like foliage... obtains favor from the Lord... cannot be moved... the house of the righteous will stand... will come through trouble... no grave trouble will overtake [him]." As for the wicked, they will receive the direct contrast (vv. 11:28; 12:2, 3, 7, 13, 21).

Third Prophecy — Isaiah 66:10–24

Perpetuating their name and posterity: In this prophecy, God comforts His people with His great blessings to the church: "Behold, I will extend peace to her like a river, and the glory of the Gentiles like a flowing stream." After pouring out the anger of His fury on the wicked, He proceeds to reveal His new church's perpetuity: "'For as the new heavens and the new earth which I will make shall remain before Me,' says the Lord, 'So shall your descendants and your name remain'" (vv. 12, 22).

Fourth Prophecy Job 42:7–17

Blessing their end: In this prophecy, He pours out the fury of His wrath on Job's three friends because they did not speak rightly of Him as Job did. He commanded them to offer Him burnt offerings, and for Job to intercede for them in prayer before the Almighty so that He does not repay them according to their foolishness. Finally, God blesses Job more than before: "After this Job lived one hundred and forty years, and saw his children and grandchildren for four generations. So Job died, old and full of days" (v. 24).

PSALMS AND GOSPELS

Matins Psalm Psalms 98:5–6

The start of this psalm urges the faithful to sing to God for choosing them at His Second Coming (as mentioned in the accompanying gospel passage), and in the second half, it points to the sound of the trumpet preceding His Coming: "Sing to the Lord with the harp, with the harp and the sound of a psalm, with trumpets and the sound of a horn."

Matins Gospel Luke 17:20–37

This passage speaks of the Savior choosing the ones prepared for His second coming, as He spoke to His disciples of His sudden coming: "I tell you, in that night there will be two men in one bed: the one will be taken and the other will be left" (v. 34).

Liturgy Psalm Psalms 98:8–9

This psalm speaks of His second coming (mentioned in the accompanying gospel passage), and the just judgment passed for the destruction of Jerusalem for rejecting the Gospel message: "Let the hills be joyful together before the Lord, for He is coming to judge the earth. With righteousness He shall judge the world, and the peoples with equity."

Liturgy Gospel Luke 13:31–35

In this passage, the Savior judges those who reject the salvation offered to them, as He told the Jews of Jerusalem whom He tried to reconcile, first by the prophets and those whom He sent, and second by Himself, but they were not willing: "See! Your house is left to you desolate; and assuredly, I say to you, you shall not see Me until the time comes when you say, 'Blessed is He who comes in the name of the Lord!'" (v. 35).

EPISTLES

The Pauline Epistle 2 Timothy 3:1–4:5

Urging them to fulfill the ministry: In this passage, the apostle describes the perilous times to come in the last days, describing the opponents of the truth, and mentioning that they will increase to an even worse state. Commanding Timothy, his disciple, to remain steadfast in the teachings he received from him, he charges Timothy: "Before God and the Lord Jesus Christ, who will judge the living and the dead at His appearing and His kingdom," to preach the word and fulfill his ministry: "But you be watchful in all things, endure afflictions, do the work of an evangelist, fulfill your ministry" (vv. 4:1, 5).

The Catholic Epistle James 5:7–16

Enduring hardships: Here, James charges the faithful to be patient in the ministry until the Judge's coming, enduring its hardships like the prophets: "My brethren, take the prophets, who spoke in the name of the Lord, as an example of suffering and patience," and giving as an example the patience of Job and God's reward, because He is very merciful and compassionate (v. 10).

The Acts Acts 15:1–18

Visiting the Gentiles: This passage shows the dispute that arose regarding the issue of circumcising the Gentiles, so the apostles and the priests gathered to look into this matter, and James gave an address passing judgment on this matter: "Simon has declared how God at the first visited the Gentiles to take out of them a people for His name. And with this the words of the prophets agree... So that the rest of mankind may seek the Lord, even all the Gentiles who are called by My name" (vv. 14–17).

SEVENTH WEEK – SATURDAY
BLESSINGS OF THE SAVIOR[44]

Linking the Readings:

All the readings of this day center on one theme: **The blessings of the Savior**—His blessings to all who have faith in His might

The first prophecy speaks of **God's blessings to the faithful**, as Jacob-Israel blessed his sons Judah and Joseph. The second prophecy speaks of **Him consoling them**, as He said on the tongue of Isaiah that "those who wait on the Lord shall renew their strength." The third prophecy speaks of **them singing of His salvation**, as Zephaniah the prophet commanded the daughter of Zion to praise because "the Lord your God in your midst, the Mighty One, will save." The fourth prophecy speaks of **His promises to them**, as Zechariah the prophet mentioned in saying that the Lord preferred the children of Zion and He is the one who will defend and shield them.

The Matins Gospel speaks of **His salvation for them** as the Lord told the blind man that his faith had saved him; while the Liturgy Gospel speaks of **His blessings to them**, as He told Martha the sister of Lazarus, "Did I not say to you that if you would believe you would see the glory of God?"

The Pauline Epistle speaks of **believers being glorified in ministry**, as the apostle said that he preaches not in human wisdom but in "the wisdom of God in a mystery, the hidden wisdom which God ordained before the ages for our glory." In the Catholic Epistle, Peter reveals that they are **being founded on Christ**; as God laid in Zion a chief cornerstone, and he who believes on Him will by no means be put to

[44] This day is known as Lazarus Saturday, as the Gospel of raising him from the dead is read in the morning, and in the evening the Gospel refers to the banquet he and his family held in honor of the Savior, before the Feast by six days.

shame. The Acts reading speaks of them **healing the sick** as Paul healed many who were sick.

PROPHECIES

First Prophecy — Genesis 49:1–28

God's blessings to the faithful: This prophecy mentions that Jacob called his sons to prophesy to them what will befall them in the last days, especially blessing Judah and Joseph: "Judah, you are he whom your brothers shall praise; your hand shall be on the neck of your enemies; your father's children shall bow down before you... [then predicting the Savior's coming from his seed] ...The scepter shall not depart from Judah, nor a lawgiver from between his feet, until Shiloh comes; and to Him shall be the obedience of the people." To Joseph he said, "Joseph is a fruitful bough... By the God of your father who will help you, and by the Almighty who will bless you with blessings of heaven above, blessings of the deep that lies beneath... The blessings of your father have excelled the blessings of my ancestors, up to the utmost bound of the everlasting hills. They shall be on the head of Joseph, and on the crown of the head of him who was separate from his brothers" (vv. 8, 10, 22, 25–26).

Second Prophecy — Isaiah 40:9–31

Comforting them: In this prophecy, the evangelic prophet calls out for the preacher of Zion to ascend a high mountain, and the preacher of Jerusalem to lift up his voice with might, saying to the cities of Judah: "Behold your God! Behold, the Lord God shall come with a strong hand, and His arm shall rule for Him," then he shows the Lord's awe-inspiring incomparable might. He comforts Israel by saying: "He gives power to the weak, and to those who have no might He increases strength... But those who wait on the Lord shall renew their strength; they shall mount up with wings like eagles, they shall run and not be weary, they shall walk and not faint" (vv. 9–10, 29, 31).

Third Prophecy — Zephaniah 3:14–20

Singing of His Salvation: Here, Zephaniah scatters Jerusalem's fear, urging her to shout with joy for the Savior's presence in her midst: "In that day it shall be said to Jerusalem: 'Do not fear; Zion, let not your hands be weak. The Lord your God in your midst, the Mighty One, will save'" (vv. 16–17).

Fourth Prophecy — Zechariah 9:9–15

His promises to them: In this prophecy, Zechariah urges the daughter of Zion to rejoice, and the daughter of Jerusalem to shout, because her King is coming to her, "lowly and riding on a donkey, a colt, the foal of a donkey," revealing that He will deliver to her all His promises: "Return to the stronghold, you prisoners of hope. Even today I declare that I will restore double to you"; the Lord of Hosts fends for her (vv. 9, 12).

PSALMS AND GOSPELS

Matins Psalm — Psalms 88:2–4

Speaking for the believers who receive the blessing of faith, as the blind man of Jericho whose vision was restored because he believed (mentioned in the accompanying gospel passage), this psalm confesses to God for His salvation from destruction: "Let my prayer come before You; Incline Your ear to my cry. For my soul is full of troubles, And my life draws near to the grave. I am counted with those who go down to the pit" (Ps 88:2–4).[45]

Matins Gospel — Luke 18:35–43

This passage shows that the Lord Jesus grants salvation to those who believe in Him as He told the blind man of Jericho (symbolic of the sinner rescued by his faith from destruction): "'Receive your sight. Your faith has saved you.' And instantly his sight returned and he followed Him praising God" (v. 42–43[46]).

Liturgy Psalm — Psalms 129:8, 2

The first part of this psalm alludes to the accompanying gospel passage in which the Savior promises Martha (Lazarus' sister) blessings if she believes in His ability to return her brother to life, and the second part alludes to the Savior going to Judea despite His disciples' warning: "Rabbi, lately the Jews sought to stone You, and are You going there again?" (John 11:8). Thus, it says, "The blessing of the Lord be upon you; we bless you in the name of the Lord! Many a time they have afflicted me from my youth; yet they have not prevailed against me."

Liturgy Gospel — John 11:1–45

In this passage, the Savior blesses those who believe in Him, as He told Martha: "Did I not say to you that if you would believe you would see the glory of God?" (v. 40).

---

[45] For this psalm, the author connects psalm 30:3, 11 to the Gospel reading, but here we have used the psalm from the original Coptic Katameros, therefore, his comments which were reproduced intact, might not perfectly fit the psalm.

[46] NJB The New Jerusalem Bible was used for accuracy.

EPISTLES

The Pauline Epistle — 1 Corinthians 2:1–8

Believers are glorified in ministry: In this epistle, Paul reveals that his preaching to them was not in human wisdom but in the wisdom of God; this wisdom being for their glory: "We speak the wisdom of God in a mystery, the hidden wisdom which God ordained before the ages for our glory" (v. 7).

The Catholic Epistle — 1 Peter 1:25–2:6

Being founded on Christ the Master: Here, Peter charges the faithful to lay aside from themselves all malice and all deceit, building themselves on that living stone rejected by men but chosen by God: Jesus, the Lord of Glory. He frankly declares to them that whoever believes in Him will not put to shame: "Therefore it is also contained in the Scripture, 'Behold, I lay in Zion a chief cornerstone, elect, precious, and he who believes on Him will by no means be put to shame'" (v. 2:6).

The Acts — Acts 27:38–28:10

Healing the sick: This passage shows that Paul and his companions' ship was destroyed on their voyage to Rome, and they were rescued onto the shore of the island of Malta where the natives treated him graciously. When a creature hung onto his hand because of the fire, he shook it off and suffered no harm. Thereafter, he healed many of the island natives of their diseases.

SEVENTH WEEK – SUNDAY
THE SAVIOR'S REDEMPTION
(Hosanna Sunday)

See *Insights into Holy Passion Week...*

WEEK 7: VICTORY OF THE STRUGGLE (THE SAVIOR)

			PSALMS & GOSPELS		EPISTLES		
DAY	***PROPHECIES***		**Matins**	**Liturgy**	***Pauline***	***Catholicon***	***Acts***
MONDAY: THE SAVIOR'S WITNESSES	*1* ***Prov****: Virtues leading to eternal life*	*2* ***Is****: God redeeming them*	His mercy to them	He gives life to those accepting evidence attesting to Him	*Avoiding stumbling blocks to the faith*	*Believers' mercy on the brethren*	*Their missionary success*
	3 ***Job****: Revealing His might to them*						
TUESDAY: CONFESSING THE SAVIOR	*1* ***Prov****: Faith-confessors are steadfast*	*2* ***Is****: God's promises to them*	He urges them to forgive sins	He glorifies those who confess Him	*Urging believers to prophesy*	*Urging them to Holiness*	*Suffering pain for His sake*
	3 ***Job****: Revealing His might to them*			*4* ***Sirach****: Urging them to repent*			
WEDNESDAY: FAITH IN THE SAVIOR	*1* ***Prov****: His salvation for believers*	*2* ***Is****: His promises to them*	Disciples need to weigh the hardships before beginning	He gives life to those who believe in Him	*Salvation of those coming to the faith*	*Faith with meekness*	*Uproar against them*
	3 ***Job****: Revealing His might to them*						
THURSDAY: RESURRECTION OF THE SAVIOR	*1* ***Prov****: Giving life to the faithful*	*2* ***Is****: His blessings to His servants*	The Savior glorifies humble believers	He raises them on Judgment Day	*The believers' awaited resurrection*	*Loving one another*	*Enduring opposition to the Resurrection*
	3 ***Job****: Submitting to Him*		*4* ***2 Kin****: Destroying unbelievers*				
FRIDAY: THE SAVIOR'S JUDGMENT	*1* ***Gen****: The favorable end to the believers' strife*	*2* ***Prov****: God rewards them*	The Savior choosing the ones prepared for His Second Coming	He judges those who refuse Salvation	*Urging them to fulfill the ministry*	*Enduring hardships*	*Visiting the Gentiles*
	3 ***Is****: Perpetuating their name and posterity*				*4* ***Job****: Blessing their end*		
SATURDAY: BLESSINGS OF THE SAVIOR	*1* ***Gen****: God's blessings to the faithful*	*2* ***Is****: Comforting them*	His salvation for believers	His blessings to them	*Believers are glorified in ministry*	*Being founded on Christ*	*Healing the sick*
	3 ***Zeph****: Singing of His Salvation*			*4* ***Zech****. His promises to them*			
SUNDAY: THE SAVIOR'S REDEMPTION	HOSANNA SUNDAY See *Insights into Holy Passion Week*						

Appendix 1: THE HOLY GREAT FAST QUICK-REFERENCE GUIDE

(OVERALL THEME: SPIRITUAL STRUGGLE)

	GENERAL TOPIC	WEEK	SPECIFIC TOPIC	WEEKDAYS					WEEKEND	
				THE SPIRITUAL STRUGGLE					THE SAVIOR'S GRACE	
				M	T	W	T	F	S	S
FIRST SECTION	FEATURES OF THE STRUGGLE	1	**Preparing for the struggle**	Forsaking Evil	Clinging to Good	Loving Others	Spiritual Growth	Reliance on God	Walking in Perfection	Leading to God's Kingdom
		2	**Nature of the struggle**	Struggling to Pray	Struggling to Contribute	Struggling Faithfully	Credo of the Struggle	Steadfastness in the Struggle	Trials of the Struggle	Victory of the Struggle
		3	**Purity of the struggle (repentance)**	Penitent Confession	Righteousness of Repentance	Trials of Repentance	Judgment of Repentance	Security of Repentance	Penitence Forgiveness	Accepting Repentance
		4	**Credo of the struggle (the Holy Bible)**	Spirit of the Gospel	Preaching the Gospel	Peace of the Gospel	Gospel Enlightenment	Faith in the Gospel	Keeping the Gospel	Strength of the Gospel
SECOND SECTION	FRUITS OF THE STRUGGLE	5	**Goal of the struggle (faith)**	Reliance on Faith	Faith-Ministry	Hope of Faith	Freedom of Faith	Vengeance of the Faith	Guidance of the Faith	Strengthening the Faith
		6	**Anointing of the struggle (Baptism)**	Repentance of Baptism	Confession of Baptism	Judgment of Baptism	Life of Baptism	Resurrection of Baptism	Salvation of Baptism	Enlightenment of Baptism
		7	**Victory of the struggle (the Savior)**	The Savior's witnesses	Confessing the Savior	Faith in the Savior	Resurrection of the Savior	The Savior's Judgment	Blessings of the Savior	The Savior's Redemption

www.ingramcontent.com/pod-product-compliance
Lightning Source LLC
Chambersburg PA
CBHW031946080426
42735CB00007B/283

* 9 7 8 1 9 3 9 9 7 2 6 3 7 *